TH UNDERGRAD RAILROAD

How To E.S.C.A.P.E. College With
Less Student Debt, A Higher Paying
Job, & More Financial Freedom

By

Jullien Gordon

The Undergrad Railroad: How To E.S.C.A.P.E. College With Less Student Debt, A Higher Paying Job, & More Financial Freedom

© 2018. Jullien Gordon

Published by The Freedom School, LLC.

To order copies of this book in bulk, email: jullien@newhigher.com.

Disclaimer:
This book is for informational purposes only. The author/publisher is not engaged in giving legal, financial, mental health or other professional advice.

DEDICATION

In honor of my two younger brothers, Newton and Patrick, all the students whose lives I've touched and will touch, and my daughter, Jada.

TABLE OF CONTENTS

Preface 1
  I Don't Know & It's Okay 3
  Why Me? Why Now? 4
Introduction: What Have You Gotten Yourself
Into And How to Escape 11
  Quick Exercise: Your School's Default Rate 27
  Planning Your Escape 30
  One Campus But Two Schools Of Thought 32
Evaluate: Where Am I? And What Do I Have? 37
  A $100,000 10-Cent Piece of Paper 37
  Graduate On Time & Save 40
  Knowing Your Numbers: Your School's
  Graduation Rates 42
  How To Graduate On Time 45
  Dropping Out: The $1.2 Million Drop Out Decision 49
  Knowing Your Numbers: Your Debt 52
  Knowing Your Numbers: Your Time Value 59
Strategize: Where Do I Want To Go And Why? 65
  College Ain't What It Used To Be & It Doesn't
  Do What It Used To Do 65
  The Easy Road Is A Dead End 68
  You Have It Harder Than Your Parents And I Did 70
  Are You Really Here To Learn? 72
  Are The Teachers Really Here To Teach? 76
  Are You Really Here To Get A Job? 80
  It's Not Your Fault, But It Is Your Future 83
  The Game and The Goal: Increase Your
  Degrees Of Freedom 86
Capitalize: What Do I Need To Get Where
I Want To Go? 95
  A 4.0 GPA Is Not The Goal 95
  Personal Capital: How Well You Know Yourself 98

Intellectual Capital: What You Know 102
Social Capital: Who You Know And
Who Knows You..106
Financial Capital: Who Knows That You Know What
You Know 109
Acquire: How Do I Get What I Need? 117
Why You're Really In College.....................................117
Campus Tour For Future Capital 119
The Process of Expansion Before Elimination 123
How To Grow Your Personal Capital:
Defining Success 131
How To Grow Your Intellectual Capital:
The Passion Finder 139
How To Grow Your Social Capital 155
Social vs. Successful Friends 157
How To Grow Your Financial Capital 164
   Earning Money vs. Making Money...........................164
   Avoid Credit Card Debt 167
Prioritize: How Do I Prioritize Everything? 179
Strategy #1: Class Choices 190
Strategy #2: Grade Goals 192
Strategy #3: Reverse-Engineer Syllabi 196
Strategy #4: No Free Time 199
Strategy #5: Strategic Sleep 201
Strategy #6: Leadership Over Membership................203
Strategy #7: Don't Work For Money 205
Execute: How Do I Get Everything Done? 211
How To Avoid Pulling All-Nighters 213
Is College Worth It?...215
The Afterword: For High School Students 221
The Afterword: For Upperclassmen, Recent Graduates & Graduate Students: If I Could Do It All Over Again Now 227
My 2003 UCLA Afrikan Graduation Speech 233
Endnotes..237

PREFACE

There is a new form of slavery called student debt. College is the new plantation and *The Undergrad Railroad* book is the North Star you can follow to E.S.C.A.P.E. it with less debt, a higher paying job, and more freedom. My highest intention for writing this book is to make it the most powerful book you purchase and read while in college. For almost a decade, I traveled the country speaking at over 100 colleges touching the lives of tens of thousands of freshmen during orientation. But I realized with over 4,000 colleges in the United States; it would be impossible to reach them all, every year, even if I was traveling and speaking every day of the year non-stop. Though my famous TEDx Talk on "How to Maximize College & Minimize Debt" has over 350,000 views, it is only 12 minutes and doesn't go into the depth I'll be able to go into with you here.

For those who immediately think this is an anti-college book, don't be so quick to judge a book by its cover. This is simply the researched and supported truth about college. I want students to know the truth about college. For too long, we've been told fairy tales about what college is and what it will do for us. The truth may hurt, but it will also set you free. I believe that if students know the truth about college, they will rise to the occasion. If colleges continue to deceive, then students will experience a rude awakening the day after graduation—if they graduate at all.

In short, here is my position:

1. The 6-year graduation rate for first-time, full-time under-graduate students who began seeking a bachelor's degree at a 4-year degree-granting institution in fall 2010 was 60% (the U.S. Department of Education, National Center for Education Statistics[1]) which means that 40% of students who begin are returning home in a worst situation than they were in when they left for college due to student debt and wasted time.

2. Those who do graduate are taking 5 to 6 years to do so which means incurring more student debt by paying 25-50% more for the same 10 cent piece of paper.

3. Even if you do graduate, graduating isn't enough and doesn't really mean you've been trained to do anything of value in today's Entrepre-New-Reality.

4. You must win college, not just finish it, and that means being intentional about your "freedom time" (not "free time") in between classes to grow your Other 4.0 that really matters in college and life (your personal, intellectual, social, and fi-nancial capital).

5. College is a rare and valuable four years of space and time to create the life you desire if you pursue the "dual degree"

which is your liberation arts education (street smarts) and your liberal arts education (book smarts).

I am happy to defend my dissertation outlined in this book with anyone at any level any time.

I Don't Know & It's Okay

Because the age of 18 is a marker of adulthood, we walk around as if we know everything and have it all figured out. As a freshman at UCLA, that was me, too; but that's just a facade. Everybody thinks everyone else has it figured out, and therefore nobody wants to look like they don't. Just because you don't know something doesn't mean you're lost. There is a difference between being lost and seeking. In fact, the people who navigate life like they know it all are usually the most lost. If they really had it all figured out, they would already have everything they want and desire right now. When you are seeking, you are open, asking questions, challenging old ideas, researching, listening, and thinking for yourself. That is what this time and space called college is really all about—finding yourself after almost two decades of programming.

Sometimes, we are too smart for our own good. In order to learn anything new, you must first empty your cup—and by cup, I mean your mind. If your cup is full, there is no room to pour anything new inside. True wisdom is not knowing everything. True wisdom is knowing how much you don't know. Your grades, whether good or bad, do not measure your wisdom. They measure your knowledge. Knowledge is based on remembering information. Wisdom is based on connecting with intuition—your inner knowing.

I believe that the three most powerful words in the English language aren't "I love you." Instead, they are "I don't know." When we start from a place of "I don't know," we start from a place of curiosity, and it's only from a place of I don't know that we can ever learn anything. Taking into account all knowledge and wisdom, there is only a small number of things that you truly do know. And then there is what you know you don't know. And finally, there is a greater amount of information that you don't even know that you don't know. On top of that, knowing information is just the first layer of knowing. Ultimately, we want wisdom, truth, and understanding.

Even as I write this book, I don't claim to know everything. All I'm sharing is what I do know from my own experience. If I waited until I knew everything to write, I would never write because I will never know everything. I know enough about maximizing college to help someone in college have a richer experience of college than I did. If after reading this book, you take some of the things I've written and find they don't fit, or they don't work for you, go back to doing things the way you were doing it before. For right now, I hope you can remain in the mental space of "I don't know."

Why Me? Why Now?

I'm not a celebrity. You've likely never heard of me. I'm not famous. I'm not a multi-millionaire (yet). You don't have a clue who I am, and you're probably wondering why the heck should I listen to this guy. I'll start with my story. Maybe you'll find a piece of yourself in it.

I am originally from Oakland, California. I was born into privilege. I'm the son of an anesthesiologist and an oral surgeon. I went to public school from K-8, and then I went to a private high school at Bishop O'Dowd.

Despite my privilege, all my parents' schooling, and that I was a second-generation college student, I still wasn't prepared for college when I got there. First, I had to adjust to the so called "freedom". Later we will get into what freedom really means, but I thought that the "free time" between classes meant I was free when in fact, it was costing me by the minute. Second, I quickly realized that what college meant for my parents and their generation, and for many of the faculty and staff at UCLA who were so pro-college was different for me and my generation. For them, the purpose of this space and time was about academic achievement and career preparation, whereas for me, it was about self-actualization and creating the life I desired.

I went to UCLA for undergrad where I graduated in three years with a bachelor's degree in Business Economics. Then I worked at a non-profit for two years where I ran a college readiness program before going to Stanford University Graduate School of Business where I got my MBA and my Master's in Education. **It's ironic because I used to help students get into college, but now I help students escape college.** Graduate school and undergrad are completely different experiences. Given that this book is titled *The Undergrad Railroad*, I'm going to focus on my UCLA experience.

I'm going to share with you the things that I did when I was in your seat at UCLA that positioned me to create a life of my own choosing upon graduating. Most of those actions took place outside of the classroom. And I'm going to share with you from my perspective how I would navigate college today given what I know now and looking back at my undergraduate experience. There are things that you will need to do that I didn't in the same way that there were things I needed to do that my parents didn't. The world has changed and how you use the space and time of your college experience must change if you want to be ready to win in the real world.

Today, I have the privilege of running my own online university at TheFreedomSchool.com. This is where I teach liberation arts education. I've created classes for anyone aspiring to live a purpose-filled and profitable life on entrepreneurship, financial literacy, personal branding, networking, career discovery, success principles, mindset, and leadership. These are the 21st-century skills I believe will help you succeed in your career and life.

My Life's Work started when I was at my little brother's graduation. I have two younger brothers—one who is four years behind me and another who is six years behind me. The youngest one was graduating from University of California - Irvine. I was with my family in the upper deck of the basketball arena, and the graduates were sitting on the ground floor. As I was searching the black cap and gowns looking for my little brother from above, I saw on one graduate's cap the words "HIRE ME." It was at this moment that I realized that **higher education was no longer leading students to getting hired**.

My little brothers are both smart, hard-working, and good young men. We had the same resources growing up. We went to the same great high school. Yet they were having two completely different experiences of the real world upon graduation than I had, and I couldn't understand why. One of them graduated unemployed, and the other graduated underemployed, meaning that he got a job that didn't require a college degree.

This bothered me so much that the night of my youngest brother's graduation I couldn't go to sleep. I got out of bed, and I started writing down all the things that I did during my undergraduate experience that prepared me to make a successful transition into the real world, and that list and those insights are in my other book *101 Things To Do Before You Graduate*. The list is powerful and tells you the what and how; however, times change, and I want you to be equipped with the why and the right thinking that will help you identify the opportunities that are always around you no matter what college you go to.

My little brothers are why I do this work. That is why this book is dedicated to them. Initially, the list was only 66 things, and I called the list the "Route 66" after the historic road that leads from Los Angeles to Chicago. I proceeded to post the list on my blog and share it with my network, and it went viral. When I saw how much the list was resonating with people, I reached out to The National Society of Collegiate Scholars, an honors society that I joined while at UCLA, and asked if they would be willing to share it in one of their email newsletters. After seeing it, they were willing, and they asked me if I had a corresponding presentation to go with it. At the time I didn't, but I said "Yes" anyway and they invited me to their offices in Washington, DC to present it to them. They were planning a national campaign to revitalize some of their chapters which were along Route 66 and they thought my content would be the perfect message to re-energize their chapters and complement their primary focus on academic achievement. That led to the creation of the *2011 NSCS Route 66 Tour* where I delivered 30 one-hour presentations to their members over the course of three months. My speaking career evolved from there as other schools caught wind of my message.

Some schools aren't ready for my message. People who have brought me in to speak have been scolded by higher ups because they think my message is anti-college and blemishes the brand of college that they promote but don't deliver on. As I stated in the second paragraph of the preface above where I laid out my thesis, this book is not anti-college. Given the resistance of Criminal Colleges running rackets on students, I had to find a way to go directly to the students themselves, especially the ones at the schools who would never invite me to speak there. This book is the best way for me to try to reach the masses before it's too late. This message is critical for students in college at a time when student debt has surpassed credit card debt, and the cost of college continues to rise with no end in sight.

Colleges are continuing to increase their prices because they can. At the same time, more and more Fortune 500 companies are no longer requiring a college degree for many entry-level positions. On top of that, globalization, outsourcing, and automation are siphoning off all the "good jobs" at the bottom of the economic pyramid. Unless a graduate can language what they can offer an organization that a computer can't do or that can't be outsourced to another country for cheaper, they are going to be economically vulnerable even if they've graduated from a "good school" with "good grades."

In short, college isn't preparing students for the real world. There was a time when the world needed teachers, and a college would create a Teacher's College. There was a time when a city or state needed doctors, and a college would create a nursing program, medical school, and hospital. But today there is a disconnect between education and the economy, colleges and companies.

You've likely heard the story of The Tortoise and The Hare. In this instance, you, the student, are the hare and college is the tortoise. You are this fast thinking witty individual that can access information using the phone in your pocket in 2.2 seconds. College is the slow-moving tortoise. They are big bureaucratic organizations, which means that they can't evolve quick enough to prepare you for the world that you're going to graduate into. It is one of the only institutions or systems that is taking longer and costing more despite technological advancements, especially the ease of transferring information. Unfortunately, in this version of the story, the tortoise never catches up, and slow and steady does not win the race.

Here's an example of what I mean about colleges being slow to evolve and their education not keeping up with the economy. I was looking through the course catalog of a school I was speaking at, and

I saw Textile Marketing as an undergraduate degree. You are likely wearing clothes as you read this book and those clothes were marketed to you, so textile marketing is still relevant and will be as long as we wear clothes. But to have textile marketing and still not have digital marketing as a major though we know the entire economy is shifting to online and mobile sales means that this school's curriculum has not caught up with the times. Even at The Stanford Graduate School of Business, one of the most innovative and nimble business schools in the world in the heart of the Silicon Valley and technology; there were no digital marketing classes when I was there.

Textile Marketing < Digital Marketing

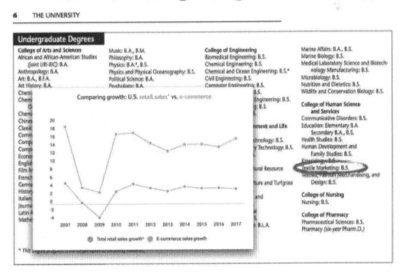

Image Source[2]

As this fast-thinking hare, you've all been told to sit on top of the slow-moving tortoise for four years, hold on as tightly as you can and let it take you to the finish line; and that once you've crossed that finish line and graduated, the doors to the world are going to open for you like heavenly gates. I'm here to tell you that this is no longer true. It may have been true for past generations, but it's not true for the younger generation today—even if you go to a *USA Today Top 100* school and do what everyone else does.

My goal is to kick you off the tortoise. I'm not suggesting that you drop out of college. What I'm saying is that there is a hidden curriculum outside of the classroom that you need to be engaged in and focused on just as much as your classes if you want to be ready for the real world once this safe and secure bubble called college bursts. There is a game within the game. The tortoise is slowing your growth and development. The world and your mind are moving faster than the tortoise can teach.

There has been a tech bubble. There has been a housing bubble. And I think the next bubble to burst will be the college bubble. At some point, the price to value ratio won't make sense, and alternative routes to advancing in life will emerge.

INTRODUCTION

What Have You Gotten Yourself Into?
And How Do You Escape?

Why did I title the book *The Undergrad Railroad*? You just got into college and have been eager to do so for over a decade. Nowadays, even some preschools claim to be college preparatory to appeal to parents worried about their children's future. Going to college is a good thing, right? What could you possibly be trying to escape from? The American narrative preaches that everyone goes to college and graduates in four years, but it's simply not true. In a moment, I'll have you research the first-year student retention rate, 4-year graduation rate, and the 6-year graduation rate for your school, and you'll see what I mean. The longer you stay in school, the more they get paid. And demand for college is so embedded in the American psyche as a prerequisite for success that your school may not even care if you drop out because there will be another wave of applicants within half a year. **In short, it's not just about finishing college—you must win college. Even if you do finish college, to finish college and to win college are two different things.**

The Underground Railroad was the term used to describe a network of meeting places, secret routes, passageways and safe houses used by slaves in the United States to escape slaveholding states to northern states and Canada. The Underground Railroad, established in the early 1800s, was aided by people involved in the Abolitionist Movement[3] and helped thousands of slaves escape bondage. The most famous conductor on The Underground Railroad was Harriet Tubman. Over the course of about a decade, she made 19 trips below The Mason-Dixon Line freeing approximately 300 slaves.

This book, *The Undergrad Railroad*, draws from that legacy. It shall be your North Star guiding you to freedom through the darkness that these institutions of "enlightenment" are in. It is the secret route to success in college and life. Instead of freeing Black people from slavery, I am seeking to free students from the debt bondage created by the higher education system in cahoots with The United States Government (Department of Education), banks, credit card companies, academic publishers, athletic apparel companies, and more accomplices. Who are they all seeking to take advantage of? You, your desire to have the American Dream, your lack of self-worth, your financial illiteracy, and the 6-figures of student loans you have easy access to as an 18-year-old aspiring college student.

In Modern Day Slavery, it's not just African Americans that are getting screwed; it's all Americans. **The higher education system doesn't care if you're Black, White, Hispanic, Asian, Native American, or anything else. The only color that matters to them is green.** All they care about is their longevity, despite their unwillingness to evolve and adapt to the world beyond their campus borders. And they are preserving themselves primarily by selling worthless 10-cent pieces of paper at higher and higher prices to 18-year-olds looking for self-worth and validation as they enter adulthood. Self-worth does not cost six-figures.

I've spoken at PWI (Predominantly White Institutions) like Randolph-Macon College in Ashland, Virginia which is 53% White, and the same racket is going on there. According to CollegeFactual.com, in 2017, Randolph-Macon has an 85% first-year student retention rate, which is great. But its 4-year graduation rate is only 52%, and its 6-year graduation rate is 59%, despite costing over $53,000 per year. As of October 2018, their website for prospective students states that:

"Currently, 95 percent of Randolph-Macon graduates complete their degree in four years or fewer. This percentage is much higher than the four-year completion rate for all graduates at private colleges (almost 80%), and for public institutions (below 50%). *(National Association of Independent Colleges and Universities)*"

Image Source[4]

This is misleading. At first glance, it looks like they are saying that their 4-year graduation rate is 95%. If they were being fully transparent, the opening sentence would read like this:

"The bad news is that our 4-year graduation rate is only 62%. The good news is, of the 62% that do graduate, 95% of them graduate in 4 years."

The 95% was derived by dividing the number of students who graduated in four years by the total number of graduates—4-year, 5-year, and 6-year—from the same entering class. Based on the College Factual data above, that calculation would be 52% divided by 59% which equals 88%. Based on Randolph-Macon's consumer information page, the calculation would be 53% divided by 59% which equals 89%. Even with these calculations, neither of those numbers equate to 95%.

Why isn't that 4-year and 6-year graduation rate at the forefront? The 95% disregards the elephant in the room which is that over one-third of students who start at Randolph-Macon don't graduate at all meaning that they return home with a mountain of debt and nothing to show for it. The 95% is an irrelevant statistic when your graduation rate is so low. A school that only graduates 10 out of 100 students, out of which 9 graduate in 4 years, could say that 90% of our graduates graduate in 4 years. Isn't it more important for you to know that the school only graduates 10 out of 100 students? The percentage of actual graduates who graduate in 4 years is a lot less significant than the actual 4-year and 6-year graduation rates.

Though its prospective students page states that 95% of graduates complete their degree in four years or fewer, its consumer information page admits that its 4-year retention rate is only 62%. The most important statistic to a prospective student is the number of students who start in a given year and then graduate four years later, not the number of graduates who graduate in 4 years. While what they are saying is true, it's intentional manipulation of language to persuade a student to apply.

There is no real system of checks and balances or accountability for colleges when their marketing doesn't match their matriculation. Just for comparison, Harvard has an 86% 4-year graduation rate and a 97% 6-year graduation rate[5]. Stanford has a 76% 4-year graduation rate and a 94% 6-year graduation rate[6].

Despite the inconsistencies between how Randolph-Macon markets itself and the truth, I do want to acknowledge that Randolph-Macon has an amazing Four-Year Degree Guarantee program which is unheard of and honorable. The website states:

Misleading Graduation Rates

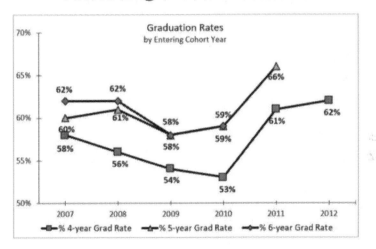

Image Source[7]

"Randolph-Macon College guarantees that if a student doesn't graduate within four calendar years, we will waive tuition costs for courses needed to complete his or her degree." Of course they are likely still making money off of housing, food, and other undisclosed fees.

Four-Year Degree Guarantee

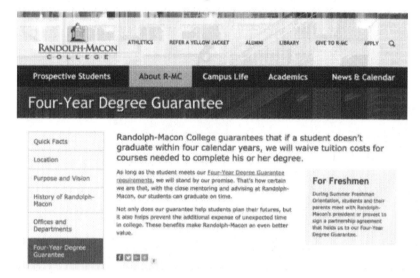

Image Source[8]

I'm just using Randolph-Macon as an example because of the huge disparities I saw in their numbers when I happened to be researching the school one day. Hopefully, this is an extreme. Go see how hard it is to get this information on your own school's website or by asking anyone in the Admissions, Financial Aid, Provost, Dean, or Registrar's Office. They likely won't know the answer even though they work there.

For the most part, students are being deceived. I wish that every school in the country had to accurately put its first-year student retention rate, 4-year graduation rate, and 6-year graduation rate on their website's homepage in a certain size red font above the fold. But instead, we make the consumer/student dig to find information that should be as readily available as the basketball team's upcoming schedule and statistics.

If there was a policy that required colleges to make that information visible, it would change everything in the same way that Yelp ratings can affect where you choose to eat, movie ratings may change what you choose to see, or hotel ratings change your decision about where to stay. But colleges aren't accountable to anyone. The federal government just started slapping them on the wrists because the default rates on the student loans that the US Department of Education issues and guarantees started to rise. That was only triggered because for-profit colleges like Corinthian, ITT Tech, and University of Phoenix took advantage of the system[9]. According to a new Brookings Institution report, over half (52%) of borrowers who attended a for-profit college in 2003 defaulted on their student loans after 12 years, compared with 26% of borrowers at two-year community colleges[10]. Now the government is threatening to not offer federal student aid to schools with high default rates, which would cripple a school's entire business model.

I see all kinds of college billboards marketing how they are the bridge into careers of the future despite their real statics. Their billboards have lofty slogans and promises that they don't currently live up to or measure.

Take the following college marketing campaign for example:

Washtenaw Community College

16% Graduation Rate

Misleading Marketing

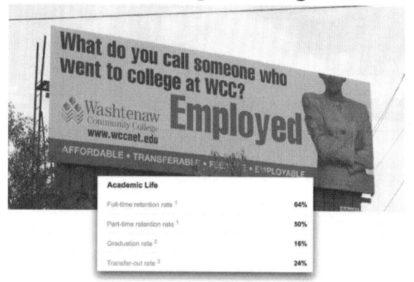

Image Source[11, 12]

But look at their statistics.

Georgia Highlands College

8% Graduation Rate

Misleading Marketing

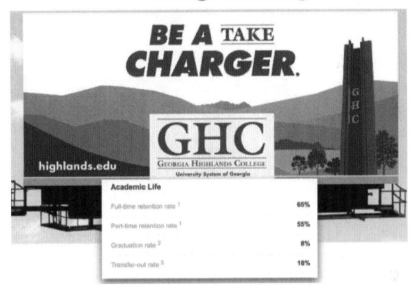

Image Source[13, 14]

Who's taking charge here? This advertising campaign won several Collegiate Advertising Awards though the school has not demonstrated an ability to graduate students[15].

DeVry University

26% Graduation Rate

Misleading Marketing

Image Source[16, 17]

There's a big separation between those who get degrees and those who don't when you're only graduating a quarter of the people you admit.

California State University Northridge

10% Graduation Rate

Misleading Marketing

Image Source[18, 19]

Seems like more of them are drowning here.

Rio Salado College

17% Graduation Rate

Misleading Marketing

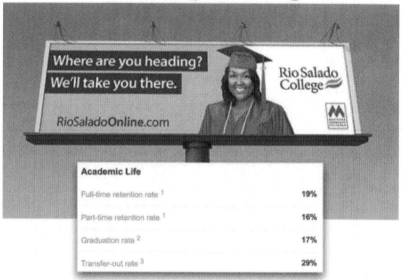

Image Source[20, 21]

Only a few are going to make it there.

The American Narrative says: be good, get good grades, go to a good school, get a good job, and success will come to you. There are young people who are doing everything they're supposed to, checking off all the boxes, sitting in the front of the class and taking notes, and yet they are still ending up over a quarter million dollars in debt when you add $100,000 in student loans, a $20,000 car note, $200,000 mortgage, and $5,000 in credit card debt. Something is wrong with this picture.

Despite their marketing and branding, which targets young people like the cigarette industry did, many colleges are what I call Criminal Colleges. They are committing the crime, but you're getting locked up in debt bondage. Their business model is so effective that college debt has surpassed credit card debt[22]. Both types of companies have the same M.O. A M.O. or modus operandi is a distinct pattern or method of operation especially that indicates or suggests the work of a single criminal in more than one crime. Both entities earn interest off your interests in advancing your life. They claim they are the easiest and fastest ways to get what you want now—a job or material possessions—and they play on your desires and lack of self-discipline. Debt is the result of trying to reap faster than you've sown. The primary reason we don't vilify colleges in the way that we vilify credit card companies is because their M.O. is masked by the mission of education. The second reason is the false belief that a college education is the only way to be successful in life.

Colleges brand themselves as these noble institutions dedicated to the education of our country's future leaders, but most colleges don't care. Usually, the trickery starts at the top of the hierarchy with the president, board of trustees, provosts, and deans. They infect key departments like admissions, the registrar's office, financial aid, housing, student life, and academic affairs. And sometimes the corruption makes its way all the way down to the professors who will do whatever it takes to get tenure and secure their jobs even if that means passing the buck to the students of the next generation.

College rankings and the race to the top only fuel the branding battles, but rankings are weighted on meaningless criteria that don't impact the student. The *US News* methodology only weights graduation and retention rates at 35%[23]. Other irrelevant factors include faculty resources (20%), expert opinion (20%), financial resources (10%), student excellence (10%), and alumni giving (5%). The graduation and retention rate should be double. All the bells and whistles don't matter if a college doesn't do the #1 thing it is in business to do. The only way to truly measure the quality of a college is to ask its current students and recent alumni. If *US News* can get the opinions of presidents, provosts and admissions deans, and high school counselors for its expert opinion metrics, then surely it can get the opinions of current students and recent alumni. These are adults. You're telling me that they can't evaluate their own experience.

The ranking of colleges is one of the only businesses where the actual consumer's opinion doesn't get accounted for. And so much of the graduation and retention data is based on the selectivity of the incoming class rather than the college's ability to educate that some higher end colleges engage in creaming—admitting the best students who were going to do well anyway with or without them. The true measure of a great educational institution is not its admissions office's ability to select the best students. The true measure is its ability to transform an incoming student into a world leader, independent thinker, lifelong learner, or engaged citizen over a 4-year period. Education should be transformative, not normative.

It's interesting that in a time when so many colleges *"strayed"* away from their original intention and lost their moral compass, that one the most malicious for-profit colleges of them all is called *"Stray*er" University. The mission of our colleges and universities has become more about revenues than results. I've traveled to hundreds of colleges and researched the corruption at others. I could put actual schools' names next to each of the corrupt strategies I'm about to mention, but each school—including yours—is likely to be engaging in several of these strategies to varying degrees right now. College graduates are estimated to earn $1,000,000 more than high school graduates over the course of their lifetime and colleges are trying to take their chunk off the top because they believe that is the value they created[24].

Here are some of the strategies that schools use to fill their pockets while killing students' dreams.

- Increasing costs through real estate investments and high-paid administrators without improving graduation rates or the quality and relevance of the curriculum.

- Intentionally making the financial aid process confusing, while also charging unexpected fees and making more aid available to students than they need.

- Increasing enrollment through athletics by appealing to high schoolers' dreams of playing collegiate sports.

- Increasing enrollment through conditional admit programs though they haven't proven they can retain those students.

- Intentionally targeting and admitting first-generation students who need the same support that student-athletes do, but not providing them the same support.

- Not offering required classes for graduation each semester so students are forced to stay longer to complete the requirements to graduate.

- Locking students into 9-month housing contracts even though their first-year student retention rate historically shows that many won't reach second semester.

- Leveraging financial aid to attract decent out-of-state or international students who pay more [25, 26].

These are just a few of the strategies puppet presidents use to increase revenues while kicking the can and passing the buck to students. They are predatory and short-term solutions that focus on the college's bottom line rather than education and graduation. With the federal government offering loans freely to students as young as

18 years old without discretion, for-profit and "non-profit" colleges are taking advantage of people's lack of financial literacy and desire to have the American Dream.

In 2017, the average student loan debt in the US reached $39,400, an increase of 6% compared to 2016[27]. Collectively, over 44 million borrowers owe more than $1.48 trillion, which is roughly $620 billion more than the overall credit card debt in the country. In 2017, the US GDP was $19.39 trillion, making student loan debt 7.6% of GDP. This type of predatory lending mimics the subprime mortgage lending that led to the 2008 crisis when the housing bubble burst. While mortgage debt was nearly two-thirds of GDP when the housing bubble burst, there was at least a real physical asset to counter some of the fallout. Student loans are backed by nothing except the belief that college is good. The $41.3 billion profit the federal government generated from student loan interest for the 2013 fiscal year is down $3.6 billion from the previous year, but it's a higher profit level than all but two companies in the world the year prior: Exxon Mobil earned $44.9 billion in 2012, and Apple profited $41.7 billion. If federal student loans were formed into a corporation, they would have ranked third in the Fortune 500 in 2012.

Federal student loans are made to students directly. And these loans are made regardless of credit history since most students don't have a credit history. To supplement the students' Stafford and Perkins loans granted by the US Department of Education, parents can apply for a PLUS loan to cover any gaps, which now puts the family in debt. At the 5.05% direct subsidized and unsubsidized loan rate, student loan providers including the federal government make upwards of $74,740,000,000 ($74 billion) per year from student loan interest. And student loans are one of the only forms of debt you can't get rid of with bankruptcy, though it's the easiest loan of that magnitude that an 18-year-old can get. More than 10.8% of student loan borrowers have defaulted on their loans, meaning that they have not been able to pay their student loans back on time.

Quick Exercise: Your School's Default Rate

My goal is not to get you to think like me. My goal is for you to think for yourself. Therefore, there will be exercises like this throughout the book so that you can see with your own eyes. Don't believe anything I tell you. Go research it for yourself and create your own understanding of college and how to utilize it to create the life you desire.

Go to this link and find your school's default rate for the past three years: https://nslds.ed.gov/nslds/nslds_SA/defaultmanagement/search_cohort_2015_CY.cfm. Identify a top-tier school in your same state and get their default rates so that you can compare. Here's an example from Cal Lutheran, a client of mine who has stellar repayment rates:

Default Rate Example

School Default Rates
FY 2015, 2014, and 2013

RETURN TO RESULTS

Record 1 of 1

OPE ID	School	Type	Control	PRGMS		FY2015	FY2014	FY2013
001133	CALIFORNIA LUTHERAN UNIVERSITY 60 WEST OLSEN ROAD THOUSAND OAKS CA 91360-2787	Master's Degree or Doctor's Degree	Private	Both (FFEL/FDL)	Default Rate	3.1	2.9	2.5
					No. in Default	37	30	29
					No. in Repay	1,193	1,003	1,130
					Enrollment figures	5,110	5,139	4,927
					Percentage Calculation	23.3	19.5	22.9

ENROLLMENT: To provide context for the Cohort Default Rate (CDR) data we include enrollment data (students enrolled at any time during the year) and a corresponding percentage (borrowers entering repayment divided by that enrollment figure). While there is no direct relationship between the timing of when a borrower entered repayment (October 1 through September 30) and any particular enrollment year, for the purpose of these data, we have chosen to use the academic year ending on the June 30 prior to the beginning of the cohort year (e.g., FY 2015 CDR Year will use 2013-2014 enrollment).

Current Date : 01/29/2019

Image Source[29]

Year	20_____	20_____	20_____
Your School's Default Rate			
Comparison School: _____			

Your school, whether public or private, is a business. The only difference is that this business is likely tax-exempt, meaning that it doesn't pay any taxes on all the revenue from you because it is an educational institution. It doesn't matter if the money comes from capital gains on their endowment, sports, real estate, or tuition, they don't get taxed. Yet at the same time, the schools are taking in federal money (aka your tax dollars) through student loans and subsidies while getting land grants to keep building. It's one of the greatest rackets of all-time and it's crippling younger generations who will have to pay in the end.

I imagine that this is how the conversation goes between the US Department of Education and colleges.

Government: Keep "educating" students. I'll happily loan them as much money as they will take at 5.05% interest in the name of higher education.

College: But what if they end up using the money for something else.

Government: Don't worry. I'll pay you directly, so you have your money. Plus, I won't tax you like I do corporations, so the money is all yours free and clear.

College: Are you sure? Most students don't graduate let alone get a job that will help them repay you.

Government: We earn enough profit from the interest even with the default rate. If they drop out, I trust that you can fill their seats within a year with a new student finishing K-12. Just keep admitting as many students as you can, so we have people to give loans to. Over-enroll like airlines if you have to. They don't all show up for classes anyway.

College: That sounds like a deal. Will do.

Your school is likely participating in a predatory lending scheme with minors. The U.S. Department of Education guarantees loans through Sallie Mae. Sallie Mae was originally set up in 1972 as a government-sponsored enterprise to service federal education loans, but as the cost of college rose and there became a gap between the actual cost and what the government was willing to loan students, they moved into private loans and became a private company in 2004. That is how your school gets guaranteed revenues and why their focus is always on increasing enrollment. **Enrollment equals revenue.**

Where else can an 18-year-old borrow $25,000 with no collateral, credit, or co-signer? Nowhere. This rare access to financing is great for your college and the government's coffers, but you get the short end of the stick unless you realize what is at stake for you. Where else over the course of the average 79-year-life can you borrow over $100,000 to buy four years of time, at a 5.05% interest rate, that you don't have to start paying back until the four years ends? Nowhere.

The next chance many get at this rare space in time of self-discovery and life design is perhaps when their kids graduate from high school; they have an empty nest, maybe they get divorced because the kids were the only thing keeping them and their spouse together, and they start anew. The infamous mid-life crisis is not worth the wait. **When we wait for challenges to come to us, they show up as problems. When we create challenges for ourselves,**

they become opportunities. If an individual takes advantage of college as I've defined it, they can avoid the mid-life crisis because they've essentially created a quarter-life crisis (if they passively wait for it) or challenge (if they create it for themselves).

I define college as four years of space and time to discover yourself and begin creating the life you desire. If you use this space and time right, you can get a 10x return on your investment. And if you use it wrong, you can end up headed nowhere fast as a result of the steel debt ball attached to your ankle slowing you down.

Planning Your Escape

There is a running narrative that you go to college and graduate in four years just like high school, but it's not true. Here are some cold hard facts according to the U.S. Department of Education, National Center for Education Statistics[31]:

- "The 6-year graduation rate for first-time, full-time undergraduate students who began seeking a bachelor's degree at a 4-year degree-granting institution in fall 2010 was 60%. That is, by 2016 some 60% of students had completed a bachelor's degree at the same institution where they started in 2010. The 6-year graduation rate was 59% at public institutions, 66% at private non-profit institutions, and 26% at private for-profit institutions."

- "Six-year graduation rates for first-time, full-time students who began seeking a bachelor's degree in fall 2010 varied according to institutional selectivity. In particular, 6-year graduation rates were highest at institutions that were the most selective (i.e., those that accepted less than 25% of applicants) and were lowest at institutions that were the least selective (i.e., those that had open admissions policies). For example, at 4-year institutions with open admissions policies, 32% of students completed a bachelor's degree within 6 years. At 4-year institutions where the acceptance rate was less than 25% of applicants, the 6-year graduation rate was 88 percent."

That 60% is the 6-year graduation rate at a "4-year" institution. Read that sentence again. That means that 40% of students don't graduate college. Not only are students not finishing college, those who are finishing are taking up to six years which means they end up paying 25% to 50% more for the same 10-cent piece of paper. As a result, they spend their 20s and 30s and sometimes their 40s trying to escape debt. These schools need to release the 2-year and 4-year language because those timelines are not common anymore.

National Graduation Rates

Percentage of first-time, full-time degree-seeking undergraduates retained at 4-year degree-granting institutions, by control of institution and acceptance rate: 2015 to 2016

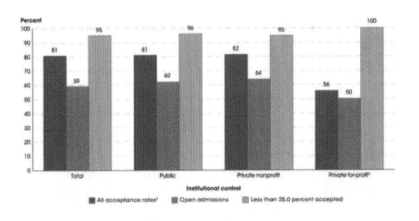

Image Source[31]

One Campus But Two Schools Of Thought

There are two institutions that exist on every college campus—one is Information Only University (I.O.U.), and the other is Freedom State. This is the game within the game. I.O.U. is based on liberal arts education and focused on information transfer. Freedom State is based on liberation arts education and focused on your transformation. Liberal arts education is about book smarts—being able to plug the right numbers into the quadratic equation and get the single right answer. Liberation arts is about street smarts—being able to approach a situation with no single right answer and generate a quality answer. Liberal arts education will cost you. Liberation arts education will free you.

Liberal Arts vs. Liberation Arts

	Liberal Arts Education	Liberation Arts Education
COLLEGE NAME	I.O.U.	Freedom State
MONEY	Costs You	Frees You
JOB	Get A Job	Create A Job
PURPOSE	Information Transfer	Transformation
FOCUS	Focused On Classes	Focused On Gaps Between Classes
BALANCE SHEET	Creates Debt	Creates Assets
AREA OF STUDY	Others People & History	Yourself & Your Story
ORIENTATION	Past Oriented	Future Oriented
MASTERY	Work For A Masters	Become A Self Master
MEASUREMENT	A 4.0 GPA	The 4 Capitals
BRANDING	Build Other People's Brand	Build Your Personal Brand
PATH TO SUCCESS	Copying & Regurgitation	Creating & Revolution
ASSESSMENT	Standardized Test	Customized Life
LENGTH	End Point	Lifelong Learning
FOCUS	Subjects	Skills
TYPE OF SMARTS	Book Smarts	Street Smarts
GUIDE	Led By A Professor	Led By Your Passion & Purpose

Liberal arts education will teach you about the past. Liberation arts education will help you create your future. Liberal arts education will teach you about historical people. Liberation arts education will teach you about yourself. **Liberal arts education is measured by the 4.0 GPA. Liberation arts education is measured by The Other 4.0—your personal, intellectual, social, and financial capital. You can enroll in both; it's your choice. Liberal arts education is how you finish college and graduate. Liberation arts education is how you win college and graduate your life.**

We often see colleges and their big libraries, their departments, professors, and research as sources of more information, as if they have sacred texts and knowledge that you can't find online or in a book. But is it the right information you need to know to become successful? If it was, every college graduate would be successful right? Why is it that some of the world's most successful people dropped out of college? Again, I'm not suggesting that you drop out. The successful people who drop out don't drop out because they couldn't hang. They drop out because the pace of college couldn't hang with them and their ambitions. If Bill Gates or Mark Zuckerberg would have waited three more years to finish college, Microsoft and Facebook likely wouldn't have grown into what they are today.

You can finish college and still fail. You've failed college if all you end up with is an expensive piece of paper. Finishing college can be worse than dropping out after comparing your debt to what capital you acquired from the college experience or not. That determines your return on investment. **What determines the value of a college degree is not the fact that you got it, but what you did to get it in between orientation and graduation.** The person who wins college won't likely be the person who studies the longest and hardest. It will be the person who invests their time the wisest in the classroom and out.

Because you're reading this book, I know that you can finish college, pass tests and pump out ten-page papers in two hours. That's the easy stuff, and that's why so many people can and are doing it just like you. In today's world, it's not just about book smarts. You need book smarts and street smarts. When you are street smart, you're able to navigate uncertainty without getting flustered. Even when there is no single right answer, you're able to find your way through the challenge ahead thanks to quality thinking and decision making.

Colleges always talk about the importance of liberal arts education. Come and get general knowledge. Learn about Shakespeare and U.S. History. Memorize the most important equations and events of our existence. The word educate comes from the Latin word educare which means to mold or train and educere which means to lead out. The education system has primarily been built on the first definition, and now it is time for the second meaning to come to the forefront if you are going to be at the forefront of the economy when you graduate. **True education isn't about depositing information into a mind. True education is about helping that mind think for itself.** That is the difference between liberal arts education and liberation arts education.

Both degrees are important. I call them the dual degree. In the past, you could have one or the other, but today, you need both. You get plenty of liberal arts education in your college classrooms. This book is designed to complement that with how to simultaneously pursue your liberation arts degree while in college. The only thing about the liberation arts degree is that there are no professors, tests, or grades to hold you accountable. It is up to you to create your own structure and stay on track to to your personal goals beyond the classroom. Even if you do manage to graduate on time with a 4.0 GPA, that doesn't mean you learned the things that are going to prepare you to succeed in the real world. I know with 100% certainty that if every college student pursued liberation arts education while simultaneously doing their liberal arts education:

- Graduation rates would go up because the bar would be higher than just finishing college

- More students would graduate on-time, some would graduate early

- Fewer students would incur increased debt from extended enrollment

- More students would get involved in student leadership and/ or entreprencurship to gain real-world experience in a safe-to-fail environment

- More students would avoid credit card debt and excessive student loans

- More graduates would have an actual skill or subject mastery upon graduation—not just a meaningless major

- More graduates would step into careers aligned with their purpose and passion after college

What if freedom was your goal after four years rather than just acquiring more information? How would you move through your college experience? What would you do before class and after class? What major would you choose? How would you choose your classes? Which student organizations would you join? Who would you seek to meet on campus and off? What skills would you develop? What subjects would you master? What books would you read outside of class? How would you spend your weekends? How would you spend your breaks and where would you go? How would you approach your grades? How would you approach work and the type of work you do? If freedom was your goal, your experience would be totally different than someone whose goal was information accumulation, and your focus on freedom would put you on a path to achieve it sooner than later. **Don't just get a degree to get a job.**

Increase your degrees of freedom until you're truly free.

Through this book, I'm going to take you through the E.S.C.A.P.E. Plan Framework. **Today, the challenge is not getting into college. The challenge is getting out on time and unscathed by debt and the deferment of your dreams.** E.S.C.A.P.E. stands for Evaluate, Strategize, Capitalize, Acquire, Prioritize, and Execute. Within each chapter, there are exercises to help you plan your escape so that by the end of the book, you have an E.S.C.A.P.E. Plan for how you're going to maximize your college experience and increase your degrees of freedom.

EVALUATE

Where Am I? And What Do I Have?

A $100,000 10-Cent Piece of Paper

If you get a CPR certification, it means that you know how to apply first aid. If you get a driver's license, it's supposed to mean that you know how to drive. But if you get a college degree, what does it mean that you can do? All it really means is that you know how to go to school, sit in a class, take tests, and write papers. Writing is the only one of those skills that has some value in your life after college. At the end of the day, what is this college diploma really worth? It's just an expensive piece of paper worth perhaps 10 cents. I have three of them—one from UCLA and two from Stanford —and guess what? I have no clue where they are. Perhaps they're in my dad's attic in a box somewhere.

The expensive pieces of paper inherently have no value. That's why so many are getting an expensive college degree with major debt and minor capital. You want to graduate with minor debt and major capital. I could go to Kinko's, get some paper stock, and replicate the diploma that you're going to receive at graduation right now. I could put your name on it, your major, your school's logo, and fake your University President's signature. If this piece of paper is what you're after, I put one below for you to cut out and frame for a fraction of the cost. Sorry I couldn't get card stock with fake gold trim for you.

Is this piece of paper what you're really after? Some graduates will get their piece of paper then they'll go to the campus bookstore and get an expensive mahogany frame for $125 and put their 10-cent piece of paper in the mahogany frame. And then they'll put it up in their bedroom and put some museum accent lighting from Ikea on it as if it's some sacred document. But if you take the frame and the diploma to a pawn shop, which one are you going to get more money for? The frame.

What determines the value of that piece of paper is not the fact that you get it. What determines the value of the piece of paper is what you do between orientation and graduation that's different, above, and beyond the person sitting next to you at graduation. If you do the same things that everyone else does, then you can't expect different results than everyone else.

College is one of the greatest hustles of all time. You're paying thousands of dollars per year to be here, but can you show me an agreement that you've signed where your college has promised you anything? Show me a document where your University President has signed and agreed to help you acquire a skill, develop your personal brand, and get a job. You can't because it doesn't exist. All they promise is to give you a window to enroll in their available classes each semester or quarter. There is no other business in the world that charges as much as colleges do where you pay without a promise except Las Vegas casinos and the stock market. So, what are you paying for? They are offering you a space, time, and access to resources and experiences. It's up to you how you use that space, time, and access.

You are investing a lot of money to go to college, and the expectation is that doing so will lead to a life of financial freedom. While that might be true if you graduate on time, with a minimal amount of debt, real skills, leadership experiences, and a fruitful career, that isn't true for everyone. You may have some friends from high school who went on to become plumbers or mechanics that will have more job security and financial security than you. Toilets and cars break down every single day whether the economy is up or down, and their chosen paths didn't require 6-figures of debt. A computer can't fix a toilet or a car by itself (yet), and those jobs can't be outsourced to another country for cheaper (yet).

But white-collar knowledge economy jobs will become more competitive because computers can think faster and more accurately than human beings. By the end of your four years, you must be able to answer the question "What value do I add to the world that can't be automated with technology and can't be outsourced to another country for cheaper?"

We think that this piece of paper is going to declare our value and open doors for us. Just because you paid a lot for your degree doesn't make it valuable. Do you know how many 10-cent pieces of paper were given out in 2017? According to the National Center for Educational Statistics, approximately 1.9 million bachelor's degrees and 1.0 million associate degrees were conferred in the U.S. in the 2015–16 academic year[32]. The more and more pieces of paper given out, the less and less valuable your degree becomes. The piece of paper doesn't increase your value by itself. How you spend your time while you're there developing your Other 4.0 is what determines the value of your college experience which we'll talk about more in the Capitalize chapter.

Graduate On Time & Save

Graduating on time is the first and primary way to reduce your student loans. It's easier said than done, but it will save you time and money that other students who aren't as disciplined and focused waste by staying in college and avoiding the real world while accumulating debt. Whenever you tell someone you're in college, they perceive it as a good thing because learning is always "good." But little do they know how much college is costing you. Don't let anyone tell you to get another degree unless they are helping you pay for it. Even then it might not be worth it because of the cost, the time, and your forgone wages by not working full-time. From K-12, we were told to "Stay in school." I'm telling you to get the hell out. While I want you to embrace the idea and identity of becoming a lifelong learner, that doesn't mean learning via expensive institutions. There are $6 books that have changed my life more than any college class I've ever taken.

The financial industry and government, who makes money off your debt, will tell you that student loans are "good debt." Student loans are not good debt. All debt is bad except debt you take on to acquire an asset. Robert Kiyosaki, author of Rich Dad Poor Dad (one of those $6 books), says that "An asset is something that puts money into your pocket. A liability is something that takes money out." For instance, taking on debt to accelerate the growth of a profitable company is good debt. Taking on debt to buy a rental property that pays you more than the cost of the principal, interest, taxes, insurance, and other expenses, thus producing positive cash flow is good debt. For instance, if you take out a $200,000 mortgage on a multi-family home and the mortgage is $1000 per month, but the rents are $2,000 per month, that is good debt. Student loans are not good debt. A college degree does not guarantee any cash flow whatsoever. Every other kind of debt, from student loans to a mortgage on a single-family home to credit cards is bad debt.

With most investments, you must work to earn the money, and then you take a risk and invest part of what you've earned into something that will give you more of what you want. In the unusual case of college, you get the opportunity to make a huge investment in yourself without working for the money you're investing. Financing college is twisted given that you don't feel like you're paying. Initially, it feels like the best deal in the world. You get to move away from home, have an all-you-can-eat buffet daily, live near beautiful people your age, wear pajamas all day, and all you have to do is take 3-5 classes. And on top of that, you don't have to pay anything until the experience is over. With most loans, there is usually some sort of down payment and then immediate monthly payments. But with college, financial aid is a whole bunch of wire transfers and ledgers. You don't have to do anything but sign your name. The hardest part is completing the FAFSA form. Once you've signed on the dotted line, you never actually see the money. It never sits in your account. All you get is the bill at the end when you graduate or drop out.

Some schools go as far as calling it a "financial award" letter to make it appear that you won the lottery, but much of the money isn't free money. It is in fact debt. And it's not good debt. On top of that, the money you get back at the beginning of the semester is not a "refund" as they like to call it. A refund is when you pay for something with your money, and you get your money back. Most people aren't paying for college with their money, so it's technically not a refund. Like a mortgage, you will get approved or "awarded" for a certain amount of financial aid, but **just because it was "awarded" doesn't mean you can afford it.** An award is what they are willing to give you. What you can afford is based on what you can comfortably pay back based on the type of career you expect to have. Therefore, you don't really know if you can afford to accept a loan unless you understand the salary trajectory for your career along with the cost of living in the city you desire to be in. I'll have you do that research momentarily in Exercise 1.5.

Knowing Your Numbers: Your School's Graduation Rates

Do you know how many kids Kim Kardashian and Kanye West have? Do you know who won the NBA Finals or NCAA basketball tournament? Do you know the lyrics to the #1 song on the Billboard Hot 100? Do you know how to do the latest trendy dance? Do you know when the next season of Game of Thrones starts (if there are any characters left with all of that killing)?

Do you know the first-year student retention rate at your school? Do you know your school's 4-year graduation rate or the 6-year graduation rate?

I think you get my point. **We know so much about nothing. Very few of the things you claim to be in the know about are helping you create the future you desire.** The fact that you likely didn't know your school's retention and graduation numbers is on you. You'll spend more time looking at a movie review on rottentomatoes.com or an iTunes review before purchasing a $5 movie than you did when choosing your college. I'm not pointing this out to put you down. My intention is to reflect to you how your current thinking about college may be decreasing your degrees of freedom instead of increasing them.

I bet they didn't tell you the graduation rates during your college tour prior to applying or at your orientation unless I was the orientation speaker. Why not? They sold you on the dorm food, the sports teams, the famous alumni, and the new buildings, which are all just cover-ups for what's really going on beneath the surface. The graduation and retention numbers should be on the homepage of every college in the country, but they aren't. They are hidden.

Criminal Colleges mask the truth by appealing to the image of college that is in your head and using nice slogans like "The Pathway to Your Future" and stock photos to entice you to enroll. Today, colleges usually reference their 6-year graduation rates instead of their 4-year "on-time" graduation rates. Why? It benefits them and hurts you. They get 50% more revenue if you stay an extra two years. I graduated from UCLA in three years, so I know it is possible to graduate in four years. It only takes seven years (four years of medical school plus a three-year residency) to become a pediatrician. Why should it take six years to graduate from undergrad?

Your school has a history and an established culture. And since colleges don't evolve that quickly from year-to-year, the most recent graduation rates you can find are likely close to the ones expected for your class. Even as you learn the graduation rates, most people assume that they will be on the positive side of the numbers. "It won't take me six years." "I'm not going to drop out." We tend to think that we are the exception to the rule. I hope that you are, but at least now you know what you've gotten yourself into and how to get out on time.

You must take responsibility for your decision to step into this experience called college without doing the proper research even though it was readily available at your fingertips with one simple one-minute Google search. These numbers are readily available on https://nces.ed.gov/collegenavigator, CollegeFactual.com, and other similar sites, and you should know them so that you know what you're up against.

Exercise 1.1: Graduation Rate Research

I want you to go to CollegeFactual.com and find your retention and graduation rates now. Once on the site, type in your school. Click the tab called "Outcomes." Scroll down to find these three numbers and write them below.

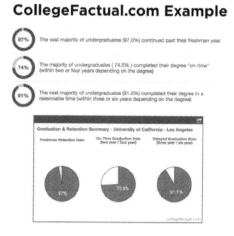

Image Source[33]

1st Year Student Retention Rate	
4-Year Graduation Rate	
6-Year Graduation Rate	

How To Graduate On Time

Graduating on time or early increases your return on investment; you simply have to map it out. By graduating on time, you'll save 25-50% for the same 10-cent piece of paper than those who take an extra year or two. In short, here's how to do it:

1. Don't stay undeclared too long.

2. Don't change your major.

3. Plan it out by semester or quarter.

4. Don't minor.

Allow me to explain in more detail.

Don't Stay Undeclared Too Long

Choose a major quickly. Staying undeclared doesn't serve you. You'll end up wasting your time taking classes that don't move you toward graduation. I know that you may be afraid of commitment. The number one hesitation with choosing a major is that people don't know what they want to do, and they feel that a major permanently puts them on a career trajectory they are unsure about. It's the belief that your major will determine your career and your career will determine your earning potential and your earning potential will determine your happiness. It simply isn't true.

According to the Federal Reserve Bank of New York, just 27%

of college grads had a job that was closely related to their major[34]. Finish your General Education courses, declare your major, and start completing your major requirements as quickly as you can. You want every class to count. I believe that you should go to college, take the classes you desire, and then name your major at graduation, but that's not typically how it works. At the end of the day, except for STEM, your major doesn't matter—your skills do.

Don't Change Your Major

Once you declare a major, don't change it. Finish what you started. Here's the reality: your major will be two words on your college diploma. Is it worth spending another year in college and paying an additional $10,000 (public) to $35,000 (private) just to change two words on your diploma? No.

We aren't even accounting for the forgone wages you would be earning if you graduated with the major you started within four years instead of switching and staying five or six years. In its most recent survey, the National Association of Colleges and Employers found that for ten broad degree categories ranging from engineering to communications, 2016 graduates are projected to have an average salary of $50,556. Don't pass up on that new money for a new major.

Let's do some sample numbers. With an additional loan of $25,000 for the extra year, plus the $50,556 in forgone wages, plus the interest on the extra $25,000 at 5.05% for 10 years of $6,893, changing your major and staying an additional year because of doing so would cost you $82,449. That's $41,224 per word if you have a two-word major like mine, which was business economics. It's not worth it.

Many people choose a major because of what their parents desire. They choose biology because they want to be a doctor or a nurse, yet they suck at science and their school has one of the most competitive nursing programs nationwide. So, they spend a year or more taking the prerequisites only to find out that they didn't get in and now they have to scramble to find another major which can take a semester or so. And then they have to start taking the prerequisites for their new major. Now they are 1-2 years behind schedule. It's a waste of time and money. Be honest with yourself about who you are and what you want and choose your major accordingly early on.

Plan It Out By Semester Or Quarter

To graduate on time, you need to begin with the end in mind. Every major has its prerequisites and graduation requirements listed before you choose it. Some courses must be taken in a particular order like a 101, 102, and 103 class sequence. So, if you don't take 101 by the second semester of your junior year, you're likely not going to graduate on time unless it is offered during the summer. But you want to use the summer to get some valuable work experience and date certain industries and companies before you commit to marrying one.

The process of mapping out your degree plan is called reverse engineering. Reverse engineer your classes for the next four years to determine what you need to take and when. This will also let you know how much freedom you have to take other classes that simply interest you. Be aware that some schools only offer required classes certain semesters, so you must plan accordingly. This is one of their tactics to get students to stay longer. Include summer sessions if they will help you finish in four years or less. Summer sessions are usually cheaper, shorter, and easier, and since less activities are going on on-campus, you'll also have time to work a part-time job to earn money to pay for those credits instead of incurring more debt.

Exercise 1.2: Reverse-Engineer Your 4-Year Academic Plan
Fill in the chart below with your general and degree requirements and prerequisites and see how your degree will unfold over 4 years.

	Year 1	Year 2	Year 3	Year 4
Fall	_____ _____ _____ _____ _____	_____ _____ _____ _____ _____	_____ _____ _____ _____ _____	_____ _____ _____ _____ _____
Winter (if quarter system)	_____ _____ _____ _____ _____	_____ _____ _____ _____ _____	_____ _____ _____ _____ _____	_____ _____ _____ _____ _____
Spring	_____ _____ _____ _____ _____	_____ _____ _____ _____ _____	_____ _____ _____ _____ _____	_____ _____ _____ _____ _____
Summer	_____ _____ _____ _____	_____ _____ _____ _____	_____ _____ _____ _____	_____ _____ _____ _____

After filling in this chart, you may realize that you don't have that much room for error. If you don't pass a prerequisite, that could mean having to wait a year to take it again which delays you getting into a major and/or every class that depends on that class being completed first. Therefore, you need to declare fast. You're not declaring your allegiance to a particular field or industry for life. You're declaring that you are going to graduate in four years by any means necessary.

Be mindful of career or financial advice from people who work at your college unless they are going to help you pay back your student loans. If someone advises you to stay longer, run the other way. As individuals, I'm sure there is no mal-intent, but as an institution, be wary. Good people can lose their sense of self when they are a part of something bigger that isn't so good, but it is offering them a sense of security (e.g., a job, health care). Faculty and staff aren't incentivized to graduate you on time. The longer you stay, the more secure their jobs are. Many have great big hearts, but most of them have only known academia. They were good students and loved college so much that they stayed in school as a graduate student and now an employee. They likely don't know the world beyond the college bubble. Education was the key for them that opened the door to upward mobility, but it is a lock for you that can bind you for two decades if you're not careful.

Don't Minor

A minor is going to have a minor impact on the trajectory of your career and life. If adding a minor is going to make you stay a semester or quarter longer, don't do it. Only add a minor if you can still graduate in the same amount of time as you would if you only had a major and if the minor really, really, really, really, really interests you. If your major doesn't matter, your minor definitely doesn't matter. If you want to learn about 15th-century Norwegian art, go buy a book, watch YouTube, or fly to Norway during Spring Break and have an experience. Don't take a class to fill your schedule and accumulate credits, when you can get the information cheaper in another way.

Dropping Out: The $1.2 Million Drop Out Decision

When someone starts college, they never think that they are

going to drop out. But the truth is that over one-third of students do. Dropping out is never a one-day decision. Dropping out is a series of small choices that culminate into a student being dismissed by the school or the student deciding not to come back. The most common reason cited by students and schools is money. Money is a scapegoat. It relieves both of them of blame because money is an external factor and deemed as a valid excuse since people perceive it as a limited resource.

From my work with conditional re-admits, I've found that the money excuse is a cover-up for deeper underlying issues like mental health (e.g., depression, homesickness, anxiety, addiction), academic unpreparedness (due to poor K-12 schooling on essential skills such as reading, writing, and basic math), skill development (e.g., time, money, and relationship management), and learning disabilities (e.g., ADHD, dyslexia). It's not that students can't succeed in college or don't want to succeed. It's that school administrators assume that because you got into college and are "adults" that you know how to succeed. In my first year experience curriculum, *The New Freshman 15: The 15 Life Skills & Success Strategies College Graduates Wish They Learned As Freshmen*, I lay out all of the success skills a student must have or develop early on to win college. What you don't have, you must acquire quickly.

The most overlooked issue on college campuses are mental health issues, and colleges are not set up to be mental health institutions. When you walk through campus, everyone looks fine. Students are wearing their campus apparel proudly and smiling with others on the outside, but there is another story unfolding. College can be a time of huge mental, emotional, psychological, and biological swings regarding sexuality, religion, and politics, and other aspects of your life.

When you were younger, you may have had all kinds of support structures to help you navigate major changes. But now, since mommy and daddy and your other support structures aren't there, you can fall into depression. In this time of need students can resort to not getting any help, trying to figure it out all by themselves, or relying on coping mechanisms that allow them to escape like alcohol, drugs, video games, etc. These big changes in your identity and responsibilities can throw you off your game and are perhaps the biggest reason students drop out. It's not that you can't read, write, study, or take tests. It's not that the academic rigor is overwhelming and you aren't capable of succeeding. It could be that the reality of life is so hard-hitting that it knocks you off your feet.

While you're being tested internally, the graded tests by your professors still keep coming week after week after week and that's how many students drop the ball. One bad grade on a test can lead to one bad grade in a class which can spiral into underperformance in a semester and so forth. How you bounce back from times like this when life isn't perfect and neither are your grades will determine your persistence in college.

The average college graduate makes on average $30,000 more per year than someone who just graduated from high school[35]. If you multiply that by a 40-year career, that's a $1.2 million difference in lifetime earnings. Therefore, dropping out of college is really a $1.2 million-dollar decision. Because we are Generation Now and Y.O.L.O. (You Only Live Once) is the theme, most college students don't have the kind of foresight needed to see the long-term cost of their decisions today. I don't want you to delay your gratification forever, but some delayed gratification is necessary to achieve your true goals and deepest desires.

Though you came to elevate and honor your family, not taking college seriously as if it is your full-time job is basically telling your future generations, "I was too lazy to study because my Instagram feed was so poppin' that I didn't have time to do what I needed to do for us. My bad." I wish that instead of putting expensive yet useless water fountains with spouts in the middle of campus, colleges put glass vaults with $1.2 million cash inside of them so that every time you came to campus, you would see what is at stake when you continuously choose your base self over your best self.

I know movies like Road Trip, Legally Blonde, How High, Neighbors, and The Social Network painted a picture in your mind of what college is all about. But that's Hollywood College. I want you to have memorable moments in college like some of the ones in those movies, but more importantly, I want you to be ready for the real world when this little bubble called college burst, and you are fully exposed by the economy, and there's no place else to hide. The economy will expose you by what jobs you can and can't get, by what type of mortgage you qualify for, and by what type of neighborhoods you can and can't live in. When this resort-like bubble called college bursts and the Hunger Games begin, where its every man and woman for themselves, I want you to be ready and ready to win.

Knowing Your Numbers: Your Debt

If you ask most upperclassmen how much money they owe in student loans right now, they couldn't tell you. Because they've never dealt with debt before, they don't know how it really works and aren't keeping an eye on it. It's like they are at the club and telling financial aid just to put it on their tab as if they have an infinite supply of money coming in from a future job after graduation. But if that money went through their personal bank account first before going to the school and they had to write checks to the registrar's office, housing office, and health department — things that are usually automatically deducted before you get your refund check — they would think about college differently.

Exercise 1.3: Monthly Payment & Total Interest Calculator

Before we go forward on this journey, we must first assess where we are. So, let's start with knowing your numbers since numbers are tangible and factual. Here is how to calculate how much what you borrowed in student loans will cost you upon graduation:

1. Go to https://www.credible.com/blog/calculators/student-loan-calculator

2. Open a new tab and go to Google and type in "cost to attend [My School Name]." Your school's financial aid website should appear in the results near the top. Click on it and see how much it costs to attend your school per year with housing, books, and other fees included.

3. Open a calculator on your phone or computer and multiply that number by however many years to expect to graduate in.

4. Paste that new number into the Home Value field.

5. Make the Down Payment field 0.

6. The loan amount should be the same as the number you typed in for Loan Amount field.

7. Type in 5.05% for Interest Rate, which is the rate on Federal Subsidized Stafford Loans. If you have private loans or a mixture you will have to do them separately and then add everything together.

8. Type in 120 months (which equals 10 years) for the Loan Term.

9. Your Total Payment, Total Interest, and Monthly Payment will automatically calculate.

Annual Cost To Attend My School (Tuition, Room, & Board)	$
# of Years I Expect To Graduate In	
Total Expected Cost of College	$
Interest Rate (%) - login to your loan provider	
Loan Term (months) - typically 120 months	
Total Payment ($)	$
Total Interest ($)	$
Monthly Payment ($)	$

Credible Student Loan Calculator

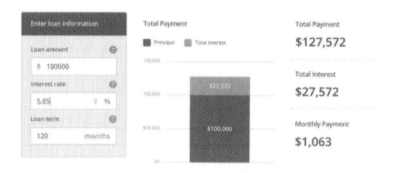

Image Source[36]

Imagine that you have $100,000 in student loan debt at a 5.05% interest rate. With the expectation to pay it back in 10 years, you will have monthly payments of $1,063 for 120 months and end up paying $27,572 additional in interest. However, the average student takes 21 years to pay off their loans. So, if you graduate at 22, that means you will be paying loans until the age of 43. That's the age President Barack Obama paid off his student loans, but keep in mind that he went to law school as well. The additional 11 years lowers your monthly payments to $645, but it causes your interest to balloon to $62,418. That's about a $35,000 difference in interest. There goes the down payment on your first home right there.

In 2016, graduates earned an average salary of $50,556[37]. That sounds good, right? It's more money than you've ever seen to date. But let's start adding up — or better yet, subtracting — your expenses. Taxes will be about $7,062 for the year, based on your tax bracket. And then we must subtract your $1,063 monthly student loan payment on the 10-year timeline. Now you're already down to $31,738 or $2,562 per month. If your rent, utilities, and internet are $1,500 per month, and then your car note, insurance, gas, and maintenance are $600 per month, and food costs you $400 per month, plus a $100 cell phone bill and $200 for fun, your monthly expenses add up to $2800 per month. That puts you in the negative by $239 per month, which likely goes on a credit card that has an interest rate between 10-18%.

If you take five years to graduate, you will spend 25% more for the same exact piece of paper; and if you take six years to graduate, you will spend 50% more. Whereas the student loan payment for someone who graduates in four years is only $1,063 per month, someone on the five-year plan will be paying $1,329 and someone on the six-year plan will be paying $1,595. Graduating college in four years has a huge impact on the financial freedom you will have once you graduate. Even the four-year graduate shown below is in the negative at the end of the month unless they increase what is coming in from their salary and other streams or decrease what is going out in the form of monthly expenses.

Post-Graduation Monthly Budget
After Student Loan Payments

Annual Cost	$25,000	4 Year Cost	$100,000	6 Year Cost	$150,000
Year	1	2	3	4	5
Salary (+5%/year)	$50,556	$53,084	$55,738	$58,525	$61,451
Taxes (25%)	-$12,639	-$13,271	-$13,934	-$14,631	-$15,363
After Tax	$37,917	$39,813	$41,803	$43,894	$46,088
Monthly	$3,160	$3,318	$3,484	$3,658	$3,841
Student Loan (4yr)	-$1063	-$1063	-$1063	-$1063	-$1063
After Loans	$2,097	$2,255	$2,421	$2,595	$2,778
Student Loan (6yr)	-$1,595	-$1,595	-$1,595	-$1,595	-$1,595
After Loans	$1,565	$1,723	$1,889	$2,063	$2,246

Exercise 1.4: How Much Your School's Graduates Earn On Average

Go to https://www.payscale.com/college-salary-report/bachelors and research your school's early-career pay, mid-career pay, and high meaning percentage (meaning, the percent of alumni who say their work makes the world a better place), the 20 year net ROI, and the annual ROI. Choose a comparison school, perhaps your school's rival or another school you were considering attending so that you can see where your school stands relative to another option.

Here is an example of what you'll see from Harvey Mudd, which is ranked #1 on PayScale.com.

PayScale Post-Graduation Average Salary Example

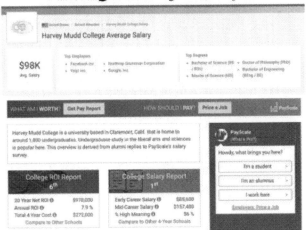

Image Source[38]

	Your School	Comparison School Name: _____
Early-career Pay		
Mid-career Pay		
High Meaning %		
20 Year Net ROI		
Annual ROI		

Exercise 1.5: Salary Projector & Post-Graduation Monthly Budget

Now that you know your monthly student loan payment from Exercise 1.3 and your early-career pay from Exercise 1.4, assume a 25% income tax and calculate how much you have left over per month after taxes and your student loan payment to pay for an apartment, car, food, phone, entertainment etc.

To find your estimated cost of living by city (excluding taxes and student loans):

1. Go to https://www.nerdwallet.com/cost-of-living-calculator

2. Type in your current city

3. Type in the city you want to work in

4. Type in your projected early career salary

5. The system will yield a number

6. Divide that number by 12 to get your projected monthly cost of living or expenses

7. Complete the table below to get your End of Month Balance

Total Cost of College (aka Student Debt)	
Project Annual Early-Career Salary (Ex 1.4)	
25% Tax on Salary	
Annual After Tax Salary	
Month After Tax Salary (divide by 12)	
Monthly Student Loan Payment (Ex 1.3)	
Leftover After Loan Payment	

Projected Monthly Expenses in [CITY]	
End of Month Balance	

This is the financial agreement you've made. I simply want you to know the truth. The return on investment from college isn't what it used to be. As their prices go up and up and entry-level salaries go down and down, you will feel the contraction. But if you use these four years to expand yourself faster than the market is contracting, you will win. The market will expose you for what you do or don't do during college. There is no way around it. You won't be able to hide behind your school's name or GPA. **The market will reveal or reward you based on how you spent your time in college.**

Knowing Your Numbers: Your Time Value

Time is your most valuable resource. People say that time is money, but it's not true. You can't buy another second of time with money. Ask Steve Jobs. Time is more valuable than money, and with only 12-16 hours of classes per week, that's what you've bought—space and time.

If the CEO makes $100 per hour and the janitor makes $10 per hour, and they both want a $1,000 iPhone, how much does the phone cost the CEO and how much does it cost the janitor? $1,000 right? Wrong! The phone costs the CEO 10 hours (= $1000 divided by $100/hour) or one long work day. The same phone costs the janitor 100 hours (= $1000 divided by $10/hour) or two and half 40-hour work weeks. **Everything costs time, not money**. Given that, you must invest it wisely in college and beyond.

Any time you are investing time or money, you want a return on that investment. In college, you either get a return on your investment, return to graduate school and incur more debt, or return home. So, let's look at the financial investment that you're making to be in college. According to the National Center for Education Statistics, for the 2016–17 academic year, the average annual price for undergraduate tuition, fees, room, and board was $17,237 at public institutions, $44,551 at private nonprofit institutions, and $25,431 at private for-profit institutions[39].

Let's look at how much these four years of space and time is costing you per minute. For this example, let's use $25,000 for one year. Now let's break that down by months, days, hours, and minutes.

$25,000 per year is:

· $2083 per month = ($25,000/12)

· $69.44 per day = ($2083/30)

· $2.89 per hour = ($69.44/24)

· $0.05 per minute = ($2.89/60)

That doesn't sound too bad. Only $0.05 cents are being transferred from your pocket to your college and housing provider each minute —even when you're sleeping.

But wait! You're not in school 12 months out of the year. You're only there for nine months. You don't go to class on weekends or even every weekday. You may only have classes on Mondays, Wednesdays, and Fridays, so we should only account for three weekdays. And even then, you're likely not in class all day on those weekdays. So, let's say you dedicate five hours per day to school even though the data suggests that it's only 3.5 hours.

$25,000 per year breaks down to:

- $2778 per month = ($25,000/9)

- $231.48 per weekday = ($2778/12)

- $46.30 per hour = ($231.48/5)

- $0.77 per minute = ($46.30/60)

So, you are actually spending about $0.77 every single minute you are on campus. **Imagine going to a two-hour lecture, but before you sat down, you had to pay the professor $93 cash. Would that change the way you showed up?** Some of you wouldn't even show up. You would try to learn the information on your own to avoid paying. But that is what is happening, except you never see the money.

What's ironic is that when a professor misses a class, not one student goes to the Financial Aid, Registrar, or Bursar's Office to request a $93 refund. Instead, they celebrate and brag about the fact that their professor didn't show up. Imagine paying for a concert, sitting in your seat, the artist canceling, and then bragging on social media that they didn't perform. That doesn't make any sense. **Higher education is the only business that we celebrate rather than complain when we don't get what we paid for.**

Exercise 1.6: Cost Per Minute Calculator

Now it's your turn to find out how much college costs you per minute. I want you to do the exact same calculation for your school. Enter in your annual tuition, number of months you are in school, how many days per week you have classes, and how long those classes are on average each day and calculate the cost of college per minute.

	Per year	$_____ , _____	Per year
	months/year		months/year
	days/month		days/month
	hours/day		hours/day
60	minutes/hour		minutes/hour

In the example above, time is costing you $0.77 a minute. Do you know that if you could figure out a business that got other people to put $0.77 into your bank account every minute, even when you're sleeping, you would earn $404,712 (= 365 days x 24 hours/day x 60 minutes/hour x $0.77 cents/minute) in a year? What if you spent four years thinking about how to crack that code instead of four years trying to graduate? Graduating is the bare minimum. It should be the byproduct of the other amazing things you do during this time.

So many students waste time sleeping in, watching Netflix, hanging out on the quad, playing video games, dating, scrolling through social media, and procrastinating on their dreams. Think about what some of your parents are doing while you're sleeping. They are out there busting their asses, slaving, trying to help you pay for college, while your ass is asleep. That is 100% disrespect. Many students' parents are slaving so that their children can have these four years of semi-freedom to create a life that leaves them better off than they are.

You're not paying for college. You're investing in yourself and your future. And the truth is that a lot of people wouldn't even bet on themselves, yet they want a company or client to bet on them once they have this expensive college degree with major debt and minor capital. As I stated before, just because you paid a lot for something or it took you a long time to get it doesn't make it valuable, and that includes your education. A college degree is simply a signal to companies that you might be good at following directions and turning in work on time. That signal was strong when we were moving from the industrial economy to the information economy, but that signal is getting weaker and weaker.

STRATEGIZE

Where Do I Want To Go And Why?

College Ain't What It Used To Be & It Doesn't Do What It Used To Do

Imagine that two people are about to run a marathon. There are all kinds of reasons we can run a marathon. We can run a marathon for a fitness goal. We could do it because it's on our bucket list. We could do it to raise money for a cause. We can run a marathon just to finish and say we did it. Or we could run a marathon to win. If one person is running to win and the other person is running to finish, will they run the same race?

No. They're going to run different races in the same marathon. The person who's just running to finish will probably start training a few weeks before; they won't change their diet or exercise plan, they won't even go check out or practice at the run's course. They'll probably train by running around their block trying to work up to half a marathon; then they'll show up on race day, run half a marathon, and pray they can run another half marathon in the same day before the finish line comes down.

The person who is running to win will start training months before. They will change their diet and their fitness regimen. They're not just going to run; they're going to do weight training as well. They'll probably run the actual course prior to the day of the marathon, memorize it, know where the twists and turns are, how much water they're going to take in and when, and where they're going to accelerate. They are going to have a strategy for the entire race.

Their intentions will shape the way they prepare for and run in the race. The x-factor to success is knowing your why. If you went to college because you were "supposed to" and you don't have a clear intention, that vague why is shaping the way you show up every single day. People who are here to win are navigating the same space and time, but they are looking for opportunities on bulletin boards, they're meeting faculty and staff, they're applying for scholarships, they are applying for study abroad programs and internships, and they're running for a student leadership position.

Winning college will create momentum in your life after college that simply finishing college will not. In the past, finishing college opened tons of new doors and opportunities for a new graduate, but that is no longer the case. It used to be a guaranteed pathway to a "good" job. Originally, most colleges were created to train you for a particular profession, but as the economy changed faster than the colleges could keep up, they moved towards more liberal arts. But today, liberal arts education is not liberating graduates—it's oppressing them with student loans.

Why are you here? Why did you come to college? What did you hope to gain over the next four years? Did someone make you come? Did you even consider another path? What do you think would have happened if you didn't go to college? On your application, you probably wrote some poetic B.S. in your purpose statement to get into college, "I want to discover myself, expand my horizons, and find a fulfilling career and I think [YOUR COLLEGE NAME HERE] is the perfect place to do that. Blah blah blah..." Does that sound about right? But once you get in and start, you have to revisit your reason why because you're a different person and you know more now than you knew when you applied.

Exercise 2.1: Highest Intention For Higher Education

Many students go to college because they think they are "supposed to." Your intention shapes the way you navigate college. Take a moment to define your why. Start with your most surface level reason by answering the first 'why' question and keep going until you get to the fifth one. By the end, you should reach your highest intention or the real reason why you are going to college.

1. Why are you going to college?

_____

_____

2. Why does that matter?

_____

_____

3. So what?

_____

_____

4. And why is that important?

_____

_____

5. But why? (Your Highest Intention)

_____

_____

In order to create a strategy, you need to know the game you're playing and the goal of the game—which is your why. As I've stated, there is a difference between winning college and simply finishing college. I want you to be in a position to win college. When I was in your seat at UCLA, I didn't know why I was in college. I was in college because I was supposed to be according to my parents and society. It seemed to be the natural next step after high school. "Supposed to" was enough reason to get me through the application process, but I knew "supposed to" wouldn't get me to graduation.

The Easy Road Is A Dead End

From the outside looking in, college looks like The Easy Road to success. The Easy Road is to be good, get good grades, go to a good school and get a good job. From the inside looking out, you'll realize that what they called The Easy Road is congested. You'll have to take an alternate route to success or pave your own road. We've all been taught to take The Easy Road, yet many graduates are wondering why life after college is so hard.

Have you ever wondered why they call it The Easy Road? They call it The Easy Road because it is easy. Apart from those who are in STEM classes, very few college students are waking up sweating bullets every morning because college is so hard. Of course, there are times when one procrastinates and waits until the last minute to start a paper or project, but that isn't a daily norm. For the most part, neither college or your classes are pushing you to your full mental potential. Many people know what it feels like to be pushed to their physical limit by a high school or youth coach, but they have never experienced the mental equivalent of that.

Since The Easy Road is so easy, everyone is taking it. And when everyone is going down the same road at the same time, it creates traffic. The way to avoid traffic and win is to pave your own road. Many of us are pushed down traditional career paths to become a teacher, doctor, lawyer, engineer, or businessperson as if those are the only career paths that exist. But the economy offers more options for "good" jobs than colleges train for or bring in for career fairs.

But most students today don't want to pursue the traditional "good" careers. And even if you think you want to be a teacher, doctor, lawyer, engineer, or businessperson, my question to you is how do you know? Who planted that seed in your mind? Where did you get that idea? From your parents? From a romantic portrayal on TV? From society at large? You can only know what you want to do as a profession if you've done the work for an extended period of time through an internship or apprenticeship. Some of us are just picking careers because they are deemed safe, secure and sexy to others. Others have chosen a career totally based on the income potential. And some of us have chosen careers because of what our parents want for us. When are you going to step into your life and start directing it where you ultimately want to go?

Instead of making such a big decision based on imperfect information, why not conduct informational interviews with alumni already doing it? Get the real deal—the good, the bad, and the ugly. A lot of people believe that a college degree is a great fall back or backup plan. Completing college does say something about you. It says that you know how to do what you're told, follow rules, and turn in things on time. There are some jobs that just need warm bodies and would value that. **I'm concerned about your joy more than your job. Proponents of college will say things like "Nobody can take your education from you," but they don't tell you that the wrong education can take you nowhere and given how expensive it is today, it can take away your freedom.**

Over this next four years, you must educate yourself about yourself. You must uncover your hopes, dreams, fears, passions, risk-tolerance, limiting beliefs, strengths, conditions of success, and your low-performance habits. This is what it means to know thyself. Life is not about who can race down an existing road faster than others only to find that you didn't want to be where that road led you or the prize at the end. In college, you have the space and time to pave your own road toward the life you truly desire rather than picking a path from a limited set of options like a multiple-choice test. This requires a deep understanding of who you really are and what you really want. You must know yourself and pursue self-mastery, not just subject mastery. **Ultimately, who you are should define what you do. What you do shouldn't define who you are.**

You Have It Harder Than Your Parents And I Did

When the Gen X and Baby Boomer generations were considering college, The Easy Road worked, but they won't tell you how easy they had it compared to you. Instead, they will tell you stories about how they had to walk to school barefoot 10 miles both ways uphill. How do you walk uphill both ways? Lies!

The truth is that all they had to do was compete against the person to the left and right of them in their high school classroom and they would be okay. Whether they went to college or not, they would still be able to own a home, get a Toyota Camry, and have two kids just like the American Dream scripted. You can ask anyone from those generations if they would trade places with you right now and they will all answer "No." Why? Because they intuitively know that the world you have to navigate and compete in is much harder than the one they had to.

I'm on the older end of the Millennial Generation, and I had to compete against all the students in the state of California. Because of my SATs, my GPA, honor classes, my AP exams, and extracurricular activities I was able to get into UCLA which is one of the top schools in the University of California system and country. My parents only had to compete against their high school classroom.

Now for you and my little brothers, the game has changed even more. You are now competing against everyone in your age group in the entire world. You have to figure out how you're going to stand out like a sore thumb among millions of graduates graduating the same time as you all over the world from equal or better institutions, with equal or better majors, with equal or better GPAs. Your college degree doesn't make you different. So, what are you going to do during these four years of space and time to accentuate your uniqueness? What skill or subject will you master even if there is no major or minor for it at your school?

It used to be that just being born in the United States meant that you had an advantage over everyone else in the world. The general perception used to be that America was 1st, 2nd, and 3rd, in all these different global categories and that's why so many people wanted to come here, but that's no longer the case. This is why we have political slogans such as, "Make America Great Again" because American has fallen behind. According to the 2015 Program for International Student Assessment, the United States is 24th in Science, 39th in Mathematics, and 24th in Reading[40]. The world has caught up educationally, and their economies will catch up now that the world is flat.

On Google's corporate website, their mission is "to organize the world's information and make it universally accessible and useful." And, since they started in 1998, they've done a great job with that, and that has made the world more flat, meaning that almost everyone has access to the same information at the same time. Back in the day, during the Information Age, having more information than those around you gave you an advantage. When I was growing up, I had an encyclopedia Britannica set at home. If I had a book report to write, I could run downstairs, reference the book, write my report, and turn it in the next day. What did my friends who didn't have an encyclopedia set at home have to do? They had to go to a library. Because I had access to information faster than they did I had an advantage.

Imagine a kid in India where, as of 2014, 58% of the total population were living on less than $3.10 per day. Who do you think is hungrier for knowledge and opportunity, an Indian teenager or you? Our parents never had to compete against anyone in India or China. Today, India has more honors students than America has students in total. Interestingly, Google's CEO, Pichai Sundararajan, is an Indian boy who became CEO of an American company. This is the global economy that you will be graduating into, and you must use these four years not just to graduate but to get ready.

Are You Really Here To Learn?

When I ask students why they came to college and we get beyond "I'm supposed to be here" and "My parents made me," the next layer of answers is "to learn," "to get a job," and "to make money." Let's take a moment to examine how much learning is actually occurring as a result of college today.

How many times have you fallen asleep in class? And if you weren't asleep in class, how many times were you asleep at home while class was going on? Even if you attend every lecture and are fully awake, how much do you learn from a talking head? When you have a test that you've crammed for, the moment you turn it in and exit the room, what happens to all the information? It magically disappears from your memory.

That's why if you stop most college graduates on stage on the day of graduation and ask them to lecture for one hour on an important topic in their major most of them couldn't do it. So, you're telling me that you studied something for four years, but you can't speak powerfully about it for one hour? That means that most college students are graduating with no intellectual capital despite having a degree.

If you really want to learn, you could learn for a lot cheaper thanks to Wikipedia. Wikipedia will give you access to 95% of the information that you're given access to in college. You could buy all the textbooks and study them on your own if you have the self-discipline for a lot less money. So, let's just be real with each other. You're not really here to learn. If you are, then tell me what you've learned up until this point and what you hope to learn by the time you graduate. It's hard to master something passively. Seeking mastery is an intentional act, so declare what you want to learn beyond your major.

This is the perfect time to start working your 10,000 hours which is the required amount of practice time to master almost anything. Majoring in something and mastering it are not one in the same. Even obtaining a masters degree doesn't mean you've mastered anything. Majoring in something means that you temporarily learned it long enough to regurgitate it in pursuit of a grade. Mastering something means you can repeatedly achieve a desired result and you can teach it because you've pursued greatness.

Exercise 2.2: What I've Learned And What I Hope To Learn

List the skills, subjects or topics, and/or things you've learned about yourself so far from your college experience.

	What I've Learned So Far	What I Intend To Learn By Graduation
S K I L L S		
S U B J E C T S		
S E L F		

When a professor misses a class, we get happy. That's not the response of someone seeking to learn. You paid for it, and it wasn't delivered, so somebody owes you. But because we're not here to learn, we are happily willing to donate about $100 to the school without recourse. The fact that most students aren't learning anything in college puts you at an advantage if you are intentionally seeking to master a subject, skill, and yourself.

Some liberal arts institutions argue that the real skill being taught is critical thinking and that the major is just the vehicle or context for the critical thinking. The dictionary defines critical thinking as the objective analysis and evaluation of an issue in order to form a judgment. But how do you measure critical thinking? How does one know if their school is developing better critical thinkers than another school?

First and foremost, information is expanding too fast for colleges to keep up. The books you just spent a fortune for at the beginning of the semester were written four years ago. Then they go through an editing process, then they get published, and then they get distributed. You will learn the information as a freshman, but then you won't get to apply it for another four to six years when you graduate, and that's only if your major is connected to your career which is becoming more and more rare. Now the information is almost a decade old and has lost its relevance. The cover will say new 7th edition, yet you can turn to the same page in the 6th edition, and the content is the same, meaning that it didn't change that much, but they are trying to sell new versions of the book because they don't profit off the used book market.

Secondly, grades are determined by how much your thoughts are akin to the professor's and other leaders in the field. This is why bibliographies and citing others is so important on college papers. But true critical thinking is being able to think for one's self, not regurgitate or cite other people's thoughts. **The longer your bibliography, the less thinking you've done for yourself.** If critical thinking was truly the goal, then more students would be critical about the college institution itself and how they individually navigate it to prepare for their post-grad future.

Are The Teachers Really Here To Teach?

The question, "Are you really here to learn," begs another question. Are they really here to teach? When I used to think about college, I thought that the primary focus was students. But that's not the case at some larger schools. In 2016 at UCLA, student fees and tuition only made up 10.8% of the school's revenues[41]. What that probably means is that UCLA students are only going to get 10.8% of UCLA's attention. At Stanford, in the 2016-2017 academic year, student income only made up 15% of revenues[42]. Don't be fooled. This is not K-12. These are legitimate businesses disguised as non-profits that receive state and federal funding and tax breaks. You are a customer, but you might not be their most valuable customer. Therefore, you won't get the attention you think you deserve for the price you're paying.

UCLA

UCLA 2015-2017 Revenue Sources

Image Source[41]

Stanford

Stanford 2017-2018 Revenue Sources

SOURCES OF FUNDS FOR FY 2017-18	
Sponsored research	17%
Endowment income	20%
Other investment income	5%
Student income	15%
Health care services	20%
Gifts and net assets released from restrictions	6%
SLAC National Accelerator Laboratory	9%
Other income	8%

Image Source[42]

Student tuition or revenues may not be your school's primary business model. I encourage you to look at your school's budget to see where you as a student fit on the totem pole. It may have other funding sources such as research grants, an endowment, state and federal funding, or a lucrative business model beyond education such as NYU's hospital which accounts for $4.4 billion dollars in revenues in 2016 while tuition only accounted for $1.67 billion and grants totaled $0.8 billion. On NYU's balance sheet, their land holdings and buildings make up almost 50% of their net worth at $8.3 billion, and their long-term investments (likely their endowment) account for an additional $4.4 billion dollars.

In fact, at NYU, a group of faculty members collaborated to put together a series of pieces called The Art of the Gouge, which describes how NYU engages in a range of predatory practices to profit off students. The president's accomplices in the racket includes financial aid, study abroad, departments, health services, and housing[44]. These practices can happen at any school regardless of their high ranking and noble branding.

Here's another example from Morehead State University in Kentucky, a state school that doesn't have a huge medical center to divert its focus away from students. I've spoken at Morehead State University for several years in a row, so I know their commitment to students. Their financial documents were easily accessible online to the public as they should be. You'll see that student fees of $36,717,000 make up 48% of Total Operating Revenues. But when you add in $63,000,000 of Non-Operating Revenues, that drops the student's contribution to only 26.2%. When I was in undergrad, I thought that 100% of the school's focus was on me as a student, but schools tend to prioritize the source of their profits ahead of everything and everyone else.

Morehead State University's 2017-2018 Revenue Sources

Image Source[45]

I'm simply showing you examples of university Income Statements to say that students aren't always first. If your school's leaders put financial success above student success, you may not be your school's top priority based on how it sources its revenues. You may be your school's second or third priority. Just keep that in mind when you're not being served and supported in the way you desire or deserve. It's just business. And in NYU's case, they are now primarily a healthcare and real estate business, not an educational institution. This is not true for all schools. Morehead State relies heavily on grants and state appropriations which come from taxes as opposed to a separate business model to keep MSU affordable and support students. It all depends on the school's leadership. Every school falls on a spectrum given where its funding comes from, and I want you to Google your school's financials so that you can see where students fit into the larger equation.

Exercise 2.3: My School's Funding Sources

Google "[YOUR SCHOOL NAME] Budget" or "[YOUR SCHOOL NAME] Financial Statements" or "[YOUR SCHOOL NAME] Audit" and see if you can find its income statement and balance sheet so that you know where you as a student stand in the hierarchy.

Year:	$	%
Tuition/Student Revenue		
Total Revenues		100%

In line with this de-prioritization of the student, many professors aren't there to serve you like your K-12 teachers were. In K-12, a teacher was paid to teach. In higher education, professors have tons of requirements such as research and writing if they want ever to achieve tenure. A tenured appointment is an indefinite academic appointment that can be terminated only for cause or under extraordinary circumstances, such as financial demands or program discontinuation. While tenure creates academic freedom for the professor because they essentially have a job for life, unless they continue to innovate in the way that got them tenure in the first place, tenure can stagnate a university's growth.

Many tenured faculty get entrenched in their subject and department's importance and use research to confirm their beliefs instead of discover new insights. As a result, they lose sight of the world at large. Tenure is the primary reason why there are so many irrelevant majors still at your school. Tenured faculty are simply defending their land and their budgets even though the importance of their field and department in the real world is on a steep decline. Their research and life's work is the lens through which they look at the entire world, so it will always be important *in their world* even if it's not that important *in the real world* as it used to be.

Some professors don't want to teach. They are required to teach as part of the school's business model. They justify their jobs by bringing in revenues via your tuition and research grants. There are professors who are bookworms and nerdy introverts who love their research so much that they would rather be in the lab alone than standing in front of a classroom teaching you. This is not a knock on those who would rather be doing research than teaching. I just want you to be aware of people's priorities. You can tell which of your professors don't genuinely want to be teaching.

Are You Really Here To Get A Job?

Most students go to college to get a "good" job. By good job, I mean one that pays well, that society respects, that has good benefits and healthcare with a good company, and that has a career trajectory. According to The National Association of College & Employers, only 54% of 2015 college graduates had a job on hand 6 months after graduation.[46] Back in the day, one graduate got two great job offers. Now it's two graduates to one job offer. Even when schools report higher employment statistics, they don't account for underemployment. Underemployment is when a recent graduate or any professional for that matter has taken a job that doesn't require their level of education. Just because a recent alumni reports that they are employed doesn't mean that it is gainful employment.

How are you going to make sure that you are one of the graduates that gets the job offer? Employers don't just want to see that you have a good GPA from a good school and a good personality. That was the old criteria for getting a job. They want to see that you know how to solve meaningful problems, create value given their business model, and lead others. A profitable employee is one who creates more value than they take in the form of salary and benefits. The market will always reward someone who gives more than they take. I would happily pay you $60,000 if you could prove to me that your skills could grow my company by $100,000 in the next year.

Given that the primary goal of most companies is to make a profit, do you know what the basic equation for profit is? This is not a trick question. Write it below.

Profit (or Income) =

If you do know it, great, if you don't, that's a red flag. You want to get a job at a company whose goal is to make a profit, but you don't know the basic profit equation. Profit equals revenues minus expenses. The way you convince an employer to hire you today is by being able to articulate how your skill or subject mastery will either increase their revenues or decrease their expenses. Since higher education doesn't teach you what you need to know to get hired today, the ball is in your court.

As an entrepreneur who has full-time employees, I want you to be aware that it isn't easy to create a job. So, for you to think that companies should just give you one because you're a good person with good grades is absurd. Every job that is available is connected to solving a problem for that company. You have to see yourself as an independent consultant making a case for why you are the best person to solve that problem for them. **We are moving beyond The Information Economy into what I call The Entrepre-New-Reality where we are all already entrepreneurs. An employee is simply an entrepreneur with one big client. In the Entrepre-New-Reality, the person with the most information doesn't win—the person who can prove their value wins.**

In fact, some Fortune 500 companies no longer require college degrees for entry-level positions. In 2016, Ernst & Young removed the degree classification for entry-level positions because they could find no evidence that going to college equaled success[47]. They are basically saying let's just bypass this whole college thing because the graduates we're getting are stressed out by debt and don't have any real skills, so we have to start from scratch anyway. Since then, other Fortune 500 companies such as Google, Apple, Penguin Random House, Costco, Whole Foods, Hilton, Publix, Starbucks, Nordstrom, Home Depot, IBM, Bank of America, Chipotle, and Lowe's have followed suit. At some point, if over 250 Fortune 500 companies adopt this mindset, the balance will tip, and it will put every brick-and-mortar college that doesn't want to evolve in jeopardy.

Companies want to see three things from a soon-to-be college graduate, that you:

1. Know how to create value, meaning you know how to solve meaningful problems,

2. Know how to get money, meaning you understand their basic business model—which is how they make profit—and where you and the job you're applying for fit into it and,

3. Have led 20 or more people, because leadership is one of the most valuable skills in today's marketplace.

Companies don't hire followers first. They hire leaders first, and followers last. In some ways, a 4.0 GPA measures how great a follower you are. It shows how great you are at following rules, timelines, and directions set by people in authority. Another sign of following is signing up to be a member of all kinds of student organizations to fill up a resume. What companies really want to see is your leadership. Leaders know how to navigate diverse people and uncertainty. You have to figure out how you're going to enhance your leadership skills while you're in college. You can do that through student government, creating your own student organization, leading a fraternity or sorority, organizing events, or creating campaigns. This will set you apart from someone who just goes to class and is a member of various organizations.

It's Not Your Fault, But It Is Your Future

It's not your fault that the world is the way it is. It's our parents' fault. They created and are leading the world that you will graduate into. But blaming someone else is always disempowering. It makes you the helpless victim, which means waiting on someone else to change in order to get what you want. If you're going to change the world, you need a world of change in you. We have to look in the mirror and determine what we can do despite the people and things we don't have control over.

Here is how the younger generations are being screwed by Modern Day Slavery disguised as The American Dream. This applies to the "good" kid who did everything they were supposed to and the kid who is too cool for school.

The American Dream: Hey financially illiterate 18-year-old! Here's a 6-figure loan to go to college in hopes that you can get a job that was created by someone whose GPA was less than yours.

Student: Can I use the loan to build my own company or invest?

The American Dream: No. Never. You can only use it for college. Now that you've graduated, to celebrate your new job, you deserve a house. How about this one? You can afford it based on your salary (before taxes, insurance, and student loan payments). Granite countertops would be nice in this kitchen. Just sign here, and you'll be a homeowner. [WINK]

Student: Thank you! This is what I've always dreamt of!

The American Dream: Ha! I know! Now with taxes taking 30% of your salary, student loans taking 30% for the next 10 years, and a mortgage taking 30% for the next 30 years, you are stuck working at a job you realized you hated after one month of working there.

Sincerely,

Modern Day Slavery

84

According to Bustle's, "How The Price of College has Changed Since Our Parents Were In School," in 1975, the cost of attending a public university was $7,833 per year (in 2015 dollars)[48]. That includes tuition, fees, and room and board. By 2015, the cost had risen to $19,548. In 1975, the minimum wage was $2.10 or $9.25 when adjusted for inflation. That means that students would only have to work 17 hours per week to pay for college. In 2015, the minimum wage was $7.25, meaning that to pay for college, a student would have to work 54 hours per week—that's almost 8 hours a day, 7 days a week, for 50 weeks per year. In 1975, a Pell Grant covered 84% of tuition at a 4-year public university. In 2015, it only covered 30%.

Previous generations didn't have to deal with the level of debt incurred in one's early adulthood the way younger generations are dealing with it today. Since 1978, the cost of college has risen by 1,225%, and the cost of housing rose by 370%[49]. Millennials and Gen Zers will be contributing around 30% of their salary (a.k.a. their monthly revenues) to student debt for the next 10 plus years, approximately 30% to housing indefinitely whether they rent or own, and 30% to taxes and social security which likely won't be available to them despite paying into the Ponzi scheme. That leaves them with 10% of their hard-earned money to live off. That was not the case for previous generations. Consequently, younger generations are delaying things like marriage, kids, and home ownership because they simply don't have the financial footing to afford those things yet.

You're in college. You've committed. There is no turning back. So now what? Let's finish what you started. The best way to predict the future is to create it. You are responsible for planting as many good seeds as you possibly can between now and graduation. The more good seeds you plant in terms of acquired and applied knowledge, relationships, and diverse experiences, the more you will reap upon graduation. The fewer good seeds you plant, the less you will reap. **For some people, this will be a four-year vacation, and they will return home unchanged with extra debt baggage. For others, this will lead them to a vocation that feels like a vacation because they love the work they do. Ultimately, you want to use this time to create a life that you don't need to vacate from.**

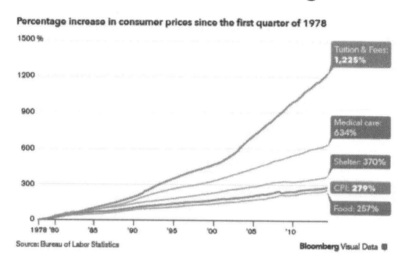

Image Source[49]

The Game and The Goal: Increase Your Degrees Of Freedom

When you graduate, will you feel freer or more bound? College is a good thing. Right? Well once the cap and gowns are gone, most students get exposed by the real world. The college bubble kept you safe. In fact, some people consciously or subconsciously take five or six years to graduate or continue on to graduate school just to avoid the real world.

No Bachelors, Masters, or Doctorate degree can save you from the Entrepre-New-Reality that we are living in. **The only degree that matters is your degree of freedom.** In the past, your level of education was your ticket to success; but today, your entrepreneurial mindset and leadership skills trump everything regardless of your education level. Whether you are pursuing a college degree or more degrees of freedom, uncertainty, boredom, and fear of failure may always be present. But if you view college as four years of freedom to create a life of freedom, the game becomes more fun.

College is a game, but the goal is not to finish—it's to win. Like a game, there is a specific time period of play, four years. There is a scoreboard which is your degrees of freedom. And there is competition—the version of you focused on getting a 4.0 GPA, and the version of you focused on freedom. There is real potential to lose in the form of student debt and missed opportunities. And there is a prize, which is your joy and success in college, your career, and in life overall.

Understanding why you're in college and how to win at college is the cure to procrastination. Procrastination is not your problem. Not having a clear purpose or a big enough why is. Once you know yourself, what you want, and why, you will be intrinsically motivated to succeed. Time is the great equalizer. We all live a 24 hour day, 7 days per week, year after year after year. None of the world's most successful people or the most successful students at your school have more time than you, yet they are yielding more with the same time. How is that so? Time management tips and hacks can help. But if you're not motivated by a higher purpose than graduation and a diploma, no time management technique in the world can save you from yourself.

I've traveled all over the country speaking at colleges and met thousands of students. I've been to *USA Today Top 100 Schools,* and I've been to schools at the bottom of the 4,140 institutions nationwide[50]. I found that **it doesn't matter what school you go to. What matters is how you go to school.** There are students who attend top schools who do the bare minimum. Their path is dorm to class, class to dorm, dorm to class, dorm to party to party to party. While their school is ranked high, they won't be when the real world exposes them upon graduation. It will be like riding the bench on one of the top teams in the country. The most you get out of the experience is the power of association, but you didn't make the team better or get better yourself. And then I've seen students go to schools at the bottom of the bottom, but take advantage of every single opportunity there. As a result, they had a richer experience of college than someone who went to a higher ranked school but did the bare minimum. If all you have at graduation is a "cap" and gown and no "capital", then you've wasted your time and money.

A people without a vision will perish. If you're the typical freshman, you have the opportunity to create a vision for your life right here and now and move toward it day by day without having to worry about full-time work, kids, food, housing, and bills the way most adults do. Most people know what they don't want, but when you ask them what they do want, they can't tell you. That's your work. Visioning means looking out into your future and creating a vivid image or set of images of the life you desire deep down inside. From there, you can reverse-engineer your path to getting there using these four years of space and time as a runway of momentum to take flight in the direction of your dreams.

Exercise 2.4: Graduation Speech

Imagine four years from now that you are giving your class's graduation speech. What would you want to say in that speech about your experience? How have you grown? What have you learned? Who have you met? How have you dealt with challenges? Use the template below to write your graduation speech. Fill in the blanks and watch your speech come together.

Class year	Good afternoon and congratulations to my fellow classmates of the class of _____
3 people you foresee helping you graduate	First and foremost, I want to thank 1. _____ 2. _____ and 3. _____ because without them, I wouldn't be standing before you today.
College name	When I first got to _____
2 feelings you had when you arrived	I was _____ and _____
2 things you were uncertain about	I didn't know _____ And I was uncertain _____ _____
High school name	I went to high school at_.
High school city	in _____. High school and college were different.

The main difference between college and high school	The main difference was _____ _____ _____
Your biggest fear about college	I was afraid that I _____ _____ _____
Your original definition of success	When I first got here, I defined success in life as _____ _____
What you want to major and/or minor in	And my number-one goal was to get my degree in _____ _____
Your new definition of success	Four years later, I've matured and now I define success as _____ _____
Something you foresee that could derail your academic goals	It wasn't an easy walk in the park. My dreams got challenged on many occasions. I didn't think my dream would be possible when _____ _____ But I persevered.
Bad grade (i.e. C, D, F)	I also remember the first time I got a low grade. I got a _____
Type of assignment (i.e. essay, midterm)	on my _____
Professor's name	in _____'s
Class name	_____ class.
How you would bounce back from a bad grade	I knew I had to step my game up. After that I started _____ _____

How you foresee paying for college	Money was also an issue. The cost of higher education was rising nationwide and so were the interest rates. To support myself financially, I _____ _____
Title 1 (i.e. President)	My involvement on campus really helped me succeed. I grew as much outside of the classroom during this time as I did inside of the classroom. I was _____
Student organization name	of _____
Title 2 (i.e. Treasurer)	And I was _____
Student organization name	of _____
Job name	I also worked at _____
Job title	as a _____
Lessons learned from your leadership and work experiences	Through these experiences, I learned the importance of _____ _____ _____
The thing you are most proud of doing in during college beyond just graduating	The one thing that I'm most proud of accomplishing during my time here is _____ _____
Why you are so proud of this particular thing	This achievement means so much to me because _____ _____

3 of your favorite items on the 101 Things To Do List	I'm also proud of how many things I checked off Jullien's *101 Things To Do Before You Graduate List.* My favorites were: 1. _____ 2. _____ 3. _____
The item that pushed you the most	But the one that taught me the most about myself and pushed me the furthest outside of my comfort zone was _____ _____ _____
What doing that item taught you about yourself	Doing this one taught me _____ _____ _____
Your first nugget of wisdom	Life begins at the end of your comfort zone. To my fellow graduates, if I can leave you with two nuggets of wisdom as you transition to your next stage of life, they would be these. 1. _____ _____
Why you believe this	The reason I say this is because ._____ _____ _____
Your second nugget of wisdom	And 2. _____ _____
Why you share this	The reason I say this is because ._____ _____ _____
Your school's mission, motto, or value	As you move on, never forget the mission of our school which is to _____ _____ _____

A thought-provoking question that everyone should keep in mind throughout life	With that mission in mind, I ask myself this question _____ _____? I encourage you to consider this question as you navigate your career and your life.
One thing they should never stop doing (i.e. being curious, dreaming)	Never stop _____ _____
Your wish for the graduates (i.e. health, wealth, adventure)	I wish you _____ _____ Thank you & Congratulations!

CAPITALIZE

What Do I Need To Get Where
I Want To Go?

A 4.0 G.P.A. Is Not The Goal

Winning has a general definition which is to beat the other team. In the game of chess, you have officially won when the other person's king is in checkmate, meaning that it has nowhere to go without being captured. In checkers, you've officially won when you've captured the other person's final piece. In basketball, you've officially won if you have at least one more point than the other team at the end of regulation or overtime. In boxing, you've officially won when you've achieved a technical knockout, the referee has stopped the fight, or you've scored more points at the end of 12 rounds. In baseball, you've officially won the World Series if you've had more runs than the other team five times at the end of nine-inning games.

When you read the specific language based on the game you're playing, you'll see that there are nuances in the definition of win. Those nuances are what inform a team's strategy. If you don't know the game you're playing, or how a win is defined, you can be working hard, focusing energy on the wrong things, pursuing the wrong metrics, and thus lose.

A specific sports example of this is when the 2015-2016 Golden State Warriors had a 73-9 regular season record but lost in the NBA Finals to the Cleveland Cavaliers in seven games (who had a 57–25 regular season record). The Warriors expended unnecessary energy on breaking the regular season record even though they secured home-court advantage throughout the playoffs already. The next best team's record was the Cavs, with their 57 wins. While it looked nice to beat Michael Jordan's 1996 Chicago Bulls' regular season record of 72-10, their true goal was to win a championship.

The 2016-2017 Warriors settled for 58 wins putting them second in the Western Conference behind the 65-win Houston Rockets. In fact, they lost 10 out of their last 17 regular season games, which I think was strategic. They turned down on the games that didn't really matter to turn up for the games that mattered most. Once the playoffs started, they turned it on, and ultimately swept the Cavs in four straight games in the NBA Finals. Their playoff record was 16-1.

Many people think that the person with the best grades wins college, but deep down inside they know that one's GPA doesn't really reflect how smart they are or how successful they'll be. Nonetheless, what gets measured is what gets done. I know the valedictorian from my high school class of 250 people, and she is doing okay. The last time I checked, she was in educational leadership which is extremely important work. But her GPA didn't give any indication that she was going to be wildly more successful than the rest of us. Winning college isn't about how you do relative to others. Since we each have a unique purpose and path, you can't compare yourself. Comparison is the number one killer of happiness. Winning college means that you got the greatest return on your investment of time and money based on your unique goals.

We've been so focused on GPA since junior high school because that could determine what high school you got into and whether you were on the honors track. And then your GPA could impact what colleges admitted you and the scholarships you earned. And then your undergraduate GPA can affect what kind of job you get and graduate school admissions. **Of course you should keep your GPA as high as you can if it doesn't take you off course from your goals. "High as you can" doesn't necessarily mean a 4.0.** There are trade-offs and opportunity costs when you seek to bury your head in the books for an extra two hours studying for an irrelevant test knowing it is only going to make a marginal difference when you could be growing your other 4.0 instead. At the end of the day, your GPA is going to be three little characters in the upper right-hand corner of your resume, and at the age of 25, nobody will care. There is a balance between academic achievement and extracurricular achievement that you must strike. Studying harder and longer may be the default, but it's not always the right thing to do.

Jack Ma, Founder of Alibaba, told his son, "You don't need to be in the top three of your class. Being in the middle is fine if your grades aren't too bad. Only this kind of person has the time to learn other skills." Robert Kiyosaki, author of Rich Dad Poor Dad, said: "One reason why your banker does not ask you for your school report card or your grade point average or what subject you majored in is that a banker is not looking for a measure of your academic intelligence." A 4.0 GPA just shows that you are great at doing what you are told to do no matter how different the tasks are. People with

4.0s are often jacks of all trades, but masters of none, while the world's most successful people get great at one or two things and learn how to manage the rest.

If the 4.0 GPA shouldn't be your only focus, what should be? I want to introduce you to the Other 4.0 that really matters in college and life. This 4.0 will be with you for your entire life, and it's up to you to grow it. There's no professor that's going to determine how high your Other 4.0 is. The Other 4.0 consists of your personal capital, your intellectual capital, your social capital and your financial capital. In this chapter, I'm going to explain what each one is and have you assess how much you already have, if any; and in the next chapter, I'll show you how to use college to acquire more capital and increase it.

Personal Capital: How Well You Know Yourself

Personal capital is how well you know yourself. When I look at you, I can't see your personal capital because your personal capital lives inside you. It's the reason people want you on their project teams in class, and in their groups: you're a great listener, a great facilitator, a great writer, or you have great ideas. It's the reason your friends want you around them: you're very caring, or you're humorous. It is what makes you attractive to others—internally, not externally.

Your personal capital includes your awareness of your gifts, talents, strengths, weaknesses, purpose, passions, interests, and habits. It also has to do with knowing what type of environments, motivators, and people you work well with and which ones you don't. There aren't many classes on college campuses that help you understand who you are, and your future employer may not care who you are because they simply want to mold you into who they need you to be. Oftentimes, you have to explore these things outside of class and do this inner work on your own through personal development classes, coaching, and challenging yourself.

The caveat to personal capital is that your personal capital often comes so naturally to you that you don't even recognize that it's actually a gift. You think that everyone can do what you do. We think "I can sing; it's not a big deal. Everyone can sing. I can write poetically. I assume that everyone can do it, too." It's not until somebody holds up a mirror to you and says, "That was amazing! How did you do that? Where did you learn how to do that?" that you start to recognize that you have a unique ability in a particular area. Listen for those words and that feedback because it is a sign that you have some personal capital that you will likely want to build your life around.

Knowing yourself is the key to success. In Ancient Khemet, (today known as Egypt), the foundation of modern-day education, above the entrance of each temple and lodge serving as an academic and scientific learning center, appeared the phrase: "Man Know Thyself." This refers to the second Latin root of the word education, educere, which means to lead out. It's not just about mastermind information—it's about mastering your inner self.

Knowing what makes you great allows you to strengthen your uniqueness. On your report card, if you come home with five A's and one F, most people would tell you to focus on your area of weakness. But while you focus your attention on your area of weakness, what happens to the things you were good at? What tends to happen is your area of weakness improves but the things you were good at decline. This is the formula to being average.

Knowing where you have gaps or deficiencies allows you to know when to ask for help and who to surround yourself with. The world's most successful people get great at one or two things, and they manage their weaknesses with their network and the help of others. It's impossible to be great at everything. And it's better to be great at one or two things than to be good at a lot of things. But the education system encourages you to be "well-rounded" when you actually want to stand out and be lopsided based on your strengths.

Exercise 3.1: My Existing Personal Capital

"Know thyself" is such a vague phrase. What does it really mean? I've broken it down so that you can really see how well you know yourself. Most will fail at this test even though it is about themselves. That's part of the point. You should know yourself better than anyone and this four years of space and time is a safe-to-fail environment that offers the best place to get to know thyself.

Write down as much as you know about yourself in each of the categories below.

Purpose	
Strengths (Take The Gallup Strengths Finder)	
Weaknesses	
Gifts & Talents	
Likes & Preferences	
Tendencies	
Dislikes & Pet Peeves	

Good (High Performance) Habits	
Bad (Low Performance) Habits	
Myers Briggs Personality Type (Find a free assessment online)	
Risk Tolerance	
Personality Traits (Visit www.ideonomy.mit.edu/essays/traits.html)	
Passions	
Addictions	
Uniqueness	
Where I Thrive & What Motivates Me	
Where I Don't Thrive & What Demotivates Me	
Values	
Fears	
Joy	

Intellectual Capital: What You Know

Intellectual capital is what you know. This includes your expertise in one or two subjects or skills. For some people, this stems from their college major, but for most people, it doesn't. How do you know if you have expertise? When you walk into any room, what subject would you feel comfortable speaking about in front of anyone for an hour? Or, what skill can you do well and replicate success more than the average person? So many college graduates graduate with majors and minors but have no intellectual capital. They're holding that expensive piece of paper but have nothing to show for it.

As professionals, we start to develop skills related to our jobs, but there is a risk of getting great at what you hate. When you get great at something you hate, you attract more of it. Instead, you might as well focus on getting great at what you want to be great at. The time commitment will be equal. Earlier, I mentioned the 10,000-hour rule. It takes approximately 10,000 hours to master something. Whether you are a student or a professional, you must be intentional about the skills you want to develop and the subjects you want to master. Mastery doesn't come passively—it's deliberate.

If there is no major that aligns with the intellectual capital you want to have, then you need to create your own major where you will study that skill set or that subject as hard as you're studying for the major your college offers, if not harder. Some schools allow you to create an independent study program where you weave some of their classes together with projects you develop. If you still want a traditional major or your school doesn't have a program like that, then you will have to double major. One major will earn you college credits and put you in major debt, and the other will earn you real money and help you create or acquire major assets.

Below is the Skills Value Matrix. It will help you identify where all your skills from microwaving to marketing events to leading diverse groups of people fit in terms of the value chain. The horizontal spectrum measures how difficult a skill is. The vertical spectrum measures how many people have the skill. I've only found one skill that many people have that is difficult to do, and that's giving birth. Unfortunately, you don't get paid for that unless you're giving birth to other people's children as a surrogate mom.

Skills-Value Matrix

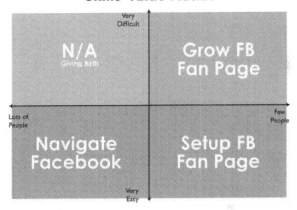

You have skills, but most of them are in the lower half of the matrix meaning that you won't be able to capture a ton of value for them. It's competitive and cutthroat below that line. You know how to write a six-page paper in 60 minutes. You know how to do some calculus. You know how to write a bibliography. You know how to take tests. And I'm sure that some of those things felt difficult in the moment. But the truth is that there are thousands and thousands of college students and graduates who have done, can do, are doing, and will be able to do the exact same things. It's the basic economics of supply and demand. The more people who can supply a skill without a change in the demand for that skill, the lower the price or value of that skill will be.

Let's say you love social media. Navigating social media would be in the lower left. Many people can do that, and it's easy. Setting up a Facebook ad would be in the lower right. Not everyone can do it. It's relatively easy, but it takes some learning. You can learn how to get an ad up in a couple hours by watching videos on YouTube. It may not be a great ad, but the basics can be learned relatively quickly. Growing a Facebook Fan Page or Group to 25,000 fans or more would be in the upper right. That takes real skill, and it takes time to learn that skill. That's why according to Indeed.com, Social Media Marketing Managers can get paid up to $100,000. There is nothing wrong with loving social media and being on it often. The question is, do you know how to solve difficult problems for others in the environment of social media?

When you think of your skill, think of it as an action or an *-ing* word such as building teams, marketing products, analyzing data, drawing still life, simplifying complex ideas, crunching numbers, or presenting in front of groups. If you choose subject mastery, get very specific about the subject. Don't just say that I'm mastering business. Get more granular in a specific component of business such as operations, marketing products, marketing services, subscription-based business models, finance, human resources, leadership development, product development, food services, or customer service. **The more specific you are with your language, the easier it will be for you to practice and pursue mastery. Your language is literally defining the lane you choose.**

Exercise 3.2a: My Existing Intellectual Capital

Consider 10 of your existing skills and subjects you feel you've mastered. List them in the appropriate quadrant below in terms of their level of ease or difficulty and how many people have that skill.

Lots of People & Very Difficult	Few People & Very Difficult
N/A **(Giving Birth)**	
Lots of People & Very Easy	**Few People & Very Easy**

Exercise 3.2b: My Future Intellectual Capital

Hopefully you have at least one skill in the upper right hand quadrant by the time you graduate. If not, you have to identify the skills that you want to be in the upper right-hand quadrant because that's where your value will be. Think about the four skills you would bank the next decade of your career on. What skills do you think will be extremely valuable in the near future and what can you do to start mastering them today? Instead of picking stocks, you are picking a skill you think will rise in value over time. List six skills you want to consider mastering below.

1. _____

2. _____

3. _____

4. _____

5. _____

6. _____

Social Capital: Who You Know And Who Knows You

Social capital is who you know and who knows you. How many people are saved in your cell phone who aren't family and are older than you? Who can you call on when you need professional or personal advice? How many friends can you call on if you need help moving? How many people are you connected with at different colleges, corporations, and organizations across the country? If you were trying to raise $50,000 for a cause you cared about, who would you call on to help you and who could you call on to donate?

Your social capital has very little to do with how many friends you have on Facebook or followers you have on Instagram. It's all about who is committed to your personal and professional growth and development and vice versa. Your social capital can consist of your friends, but all relationships aren't created equal. Higher capital relationships include mentors, alumni, seasoned professionals, parents' friends, professors, counselors, coaches, advisors, and peers committed to your personal greatness (which I call your "successful friends").

Connections and capital are not one and the same. Facebook allows you to have 5,000 friends or social connections, but those are likely weak connections. Social capital means that you can leverage those relationships and their capital for a goal that you have. Social capital is powerful because, with each person in your network, you gain access to their personal, intellectual, social, and sometimes financial capital. This is why they say your network is your net worth.

Networks can grow in many directions—up, down, across, and out. Your network across is made up of your friends. That's the easiest network to build because it is facilitated for you through your housing arrangement, group projects in classes, jobs, internships, and participation in student organizations. You may find that after college, making friends is not as easy.

Networking down means connecting with people who are younger than you such as underclassmen, your siblings and their friends, and mentees. They can keep you young and expose you to trends and things you are too old to catch.

Networking out involves getting out of your natural environment which is your college campus and actively seeking to meet people who you might not otherwise meet. This could mean joining a national student organization and going to their national convention where you meet students from different schools. This could mean finding an off-campus event or internship where you likely won't know anybody.

Networking up is perhaps the most powerful form of networking you can do right now. Networking up means building relationships with faculty, staff, mentors, alumni, community leaders, and business leaders. One relationship upward could be equivalent to the value of twenty relationships across. Your friends can get you to the door you're trying to get into, but wouldn't you rather know the person who has the key to the door or who is on the other side of the door and can open it for you? These are the kinds of people who will write your letters of recommendations for you, make personal calls to potential employers, and expose you to unique opportunities that end up on their desk or in their email.

To build these kinds of relationships, you must have The Middle Seat Mentality. On an airplane, most people avoid the middle seat because they feel squished between the person in the window seat and the aisle seat. But the benefit of the middle seat is that it allows you to easily meet two people, whereas the other seats only put you in position to meet one person. The Middle Seat Mentality means that you always seek ways to put yourself in a position to meet the most people wherever you are whether you're on an airplane, at a party, at a networking event, or in the dining hall. It's so easy for us to sit at the same table and eat with the same people at the dining hall every day, but doing so cuts us off from meeting other amazing people who are less than a table-length away from us. In the next chapter, we will cover the distinction between your social and successful friends. For now, let's evaluate the social capital you've developed so far.

Exercise 3.3: My Existing Social Capital

Think about the people who know you and have your best interests in mind. List their names below and what you go to them for.

	Know Me & Looking Out For Me	I Go To Them For...
Professors		
Staff & Advisors		
Alumni		
Upperclassmen		
Successful Friends		

Mentors		
Other People Who Care & Check-In On Me		

Financial Capital: Who Knows That You Know What You Know

Financial capital is who knows that you know what you know. Reread that—it's a tricky one. Your financial capital grows at the intersection of your intellectual and social capital. When the right people know that you know a lot about a subject or can execute a skill that they need, that's when financial opportunities flow. The reason I get paid to speak at colleges across the country is because the right people (my social capital), know that I know a lot about helping today's students succeed (my intellectual capital), and when those two things intersect, financial opportunities emerge.

Making money is not complex. However, we tend to put our head in the sand and try to get good at a subject or skill, but don't do the personal branding work necessary to let people know that we have acquired this skill or subject mastery. We hope that someone just discovers us and sees our talent jump out at them off a flat resume. When you're smart, sometimes you hide your brilliance because you don't want to be perceived as arrogant or nerdy. Hiding your intelligence may have benefited you on the social scene in high school or college so that you could fit in, but hiding your brilliance in the real world will hurt you financially. You want as many people as possible to know how great you are without being boastful. Don't exaggerate with words from the thesaurus. Allow your results to speak for themselves.

Imagine that you are looking for a new job opportunity—which is a financial opportunity—the interview process is all about building a relationship with the hiring manager, interviewers, and the company, and then convincing them that you are the most knowledgeable and skillful at solving the problem they are hiring for. Anyone who has strong social capital and knows people in their target company has an advantage because referrals are one of the top ways people get jobs. Also, those who can demonstrate their intellectual capital through past performance or artifacts and evidence of success will have an advantage in the hiring process as well because they are showing their value, not telling about it.

While a salary is a great source of financial capital, its growth is oftentimes dictated by a corporate ladder that you must wait to advance up. When you think about your financial capital as the intersection of your intellectual and social capital, it empowers you because you are in full control of how your intellectual and social capitals grow. Financial capital comes in the form of job opportunities, investment opportunities, entrepreneurial opportunities, and access to capital. If I were to ask the ten closest people to you what your area of expertise is, would they know? If not, you have an opportunity to improve your personal branding so that when people who know you meet someone who can benefit from your expertise, they think of you and make an introduction.

The more people who know that you know what you know will surely bring more money your way, but just because you know how to make money doesn't mean you know how to manage it. They say it's not what you make; it's what you keep. Until you are working in a way where you get paid consistently, you can use the management of your refund check and money from a part-time job to practice.

Every company, as well as every individual, should have a balance sheet and an income statement. The balance sheet measures your net worth by subtracting your liabilities from your assets. Assets are things you own including the cash in your checking and savings accounts, stocks and bonds, and real estate. Liabilities are things you owe including your debts such as your student loans, credit card debt, car note, and mortgage. Right now, as your student loans accumulate, your net worth is likely negative. Keep in mind that a baby born within the last 60 seconds enters the world with a net worth of zero, so it may have a higher net worth than you at this moment in time.

In the conversation with Modern Day Slavery earlier, there was a wink after you bought your home. Why? Because if you watch enough episodes of HGTV, they'll have you convinced that the moment you get the key, you're a homeowner when you're not. When you close on a home, you are a home buyer—not a homeowner. The bank owns up to 97% of your home at that time. You don't become a homeowner until the mortgage is paid in full. They call a home an asset, but referring back to Robert Kiyosaki, an asset is something that puts money into your pocket. A single-family home will only take money out. Even after you've paid off the mortgage 30 years later, you'll still have to pay property taxes and insurance plus repairs on a home that is 30 years older. A home is an illiquid savings account at best. Your money is locked into your granite countertops. You can't spend it. And homes don't always appreciate.

The income statement measures your monthly or annual income or cash flow by subtracting your total expenses from your total revenues. Your revenues will primarily be your paycheck, but in the future, it could include rents from rental properties you own and dividends from stocks. Another way you are manipulated by The American Dream with language is by calling your salary your income, but it's not. Remember that in a business, profit or income equals revenues minus expenses. Therefore, your salary is your revenue. Your income is what's leftover at the end of the month after you've paid all your expenses. Two people could have the same salaries but different incomes. Your expenses include your rent, cell phone, internet, TV, subscriptions, food, tuition, car note, car insurance, gas, parking, car maintenance, health insurance, entertainment, credit card payments, personal shopping, and other daily needs. You want more money left over at the end of the month, but most people have more month left over at the end of the money. In fact, 76% of Americans are living paycheck-to-paycheck[51].

For many college students, the receipt of their refund check was the first time they ever saw a comma in their bank account, but nobody taught them how to manage money, so they blew through it even though it was supposed to last them for the entire semester. In the exercises below, you'll calculate your net worth and create a monthly budget which are the foundations of learning how to manage your money.

Exercise 3.4: My Existing Financial Capital (Balance Sheet/Net Worth)

Log in to your bank accounts and see how much money you have. If you have other assets, add them as well. Next, go to the financial aid office or login to your loan provider account and see how much your student loans are now. Also gather information regarding credit cards, car loans, and any other debt you may have. Use all that information to calculate your net worth today.

ASSETS	
Checking	
Savings	
Other:	
TOTAL ASSETS	
LIABILITIES	
Student Loans	
Credit Cards	
Car Loan	
Other:	
TOTAL LIABILITIES	
TOTAL NET WORTH (Total Assets - Total Liabilities)	

Exercise 3.5: My Existing Financial Capital
(Income Statement/Monthly Budget)

REVENUES: First, look at your refund check which is what is left over from your financial aid after tuition and housing and other fees have been taken out. Divide that number by the number of months in your semester or quarter. Also, add in how much you get paid monthly from any jobs based on the average hours you work or any money that you are paid or gifted on a regular basis.

EXPENSES: Log in to your bank account or service accounts and see how much is being billed on average for the expenses in the table below. In some cases, like off-campus housing or car insurance, you may have paid for several months at a time, and that number has to be divided into a monthly expense.

INCOME: Subtract your total expenses from your total revenues to get your monthly income. This number is essentially your expected breathing room at the end of each month if you stay on budget.

REVENUES	
Refund Check Divided By Weeks In Semester	
Job 1:	
Other:	
TOTAL REVENUES	
EXPENSES	
Rent (if paid monthly)	
Food	

Car Note	
Cell Phone	
Internet	
TV	
Subscriptions	
Tuition (if paid monthly)	
Car Note	
Parking (if paid monthly)	
Car Insurance (break it down monthly)	
Gas	
Car Maintenance (set aside an amount)	
Health Insurance	
Entertainment	
Personal Shopping	
Credit Card Payments	
Other	
TOTAL EXPENSES	
TOTAL MONTHLY INCOME (Total Revenues - Total Expenses)	

ACQUIRE

How Do I Get What I Need?

Why You're Really In College

In the previous chapter, you defined your existing personal, intellectual, social, and financial capital. At this stage of life, your Other 4.0 may be quite low. That's okay. That's what these four years is all about. You must use this time to grow it. When you assess the difference between what you have and what you need to become who you want to be and have what you want to have, you may notice some significant gaps in your Other 4.0.

Perhaps you don't have the degree of self-discipline you think you need as part of your personal capital to do what you want in the world. Or you may feel like you're lacking intellectual capital around leadership, people skills, or quantitative skills to become who you want to be. These major or minor gaps should be areas of focus during college just like your academic major or minor. You are here to acquire what you need to become the person you want to be.

Every campus has its own intellectual, social, and financial capital that you have access to use—or not. Your campus' intellectual capital is anywhere you have unique access to information such as its courses, centers, libraries, online databases, programs, and events. Your campus' social capital is anywhere you have unique access to people. Examples of unique relationships would be professors, students, alumni networks, student groups, connections in the community, and guest speakers. Your campus' financial capital is anywhere you have unique access to money. That includes its student government, scholarships, grants, financial aid, the Career Center's access to jobs, and equipment that you have access to that other people would have to pay for.

Campus Capital

Intellectual	Social	Financial
Courses	Professors	Student Government
Centers	Classmates	Scholarships
Libraries	Alumni Network	Grants
Online Databases	Student Groups	Financial Aid
Programs	Guest Speakers	Career Center
Events		Equipment

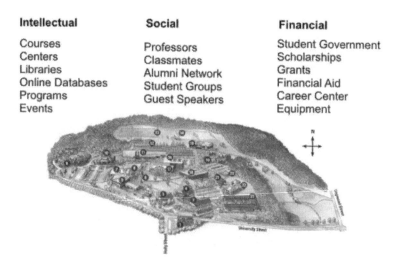

Here is why you're in college in the very simplest form: **You are in college to use their intellectual, social, and financial capital to grow your intellectual, social and financial capital so that you are more valuable at graduation than you were at orientation.** You're paying them $25,000 to come into their kitchen and use their ingredients to grow and bake whatever it is that you're trying to create. Getting into college and paying tuition gives you access. You are responsible for the acquiring part of the equation. Access. Acquire. Access. Acquire. That's the name of the game.

Here's the problem. Most students enter college and think of it as more school. To them, it's just grades 13 through 16. Everyone will graduate, especially me, just like in high school. That isn't true, and in college, there is no social promotion. Because most people come to college and see it as more school, they only focus on classes. College looks like school. You have classes, teachers, tests, books, and grades, but academics only make up 40% of the college experience. The real richness of the college experience is what takes place outside of the classroom. If you're over-focused on classes and grades, you'll miss out on leadership, work, and growth experiences because you're too busy reading outdated textbooks, writing meaningless papers and studying for irrelevant tests that you intuitively know will not impact your future one iota.

Campus Tour For Future Capital

When you came to campus to visit before applying and again at orientation, you probably got the same dry campus tour. "This is the statue of the old White guy who founded our school and here is the first building. This is our sports facility for our athletes who get pampered but not paid. Here are our all-inclusive, resort-like, overpriced dorms. And here is a new building named after some alumni who gave us a few million dollars." That kind of campus tour is all about the history of the campus and has nothing to do with your future.

You must take a different kind of campus tour with the goal of identifying where all of the access points to the intellectual, social, and financial capital that can help you create the life you desire are located. From the outside looking in, it is hard to assess how much capital a campus has, but once you're there, you can uncover it with some help. Trying to map out the campus by yourself may take four years, and by then it is time to graduate. The fastest way to map out where the capital that is relevant to you is located is to talk to someone who has a birds-eye-view of the campus. You want to take your goals, gaps, and a campus map to several people who have been there for five years or more and have them point out exactly who and what you need to know. This will likely be a faculty member, staff member, or advisor who bleeds your school's colors and has a deep love for students.

Literally go get a campus map, go to that person's office and have the following conversation.

You: Thank you in advance for your time. I have four quick questions to ask you that will tremendously transform my experience and help me maximize my time. Here are my goals in college and beyond. [STATE YOUR GOALS]. Here are my gaps where I know I need help. [STATE YOUR GAPS]. I also have a campus map, so you can show me exactly where to go and who to meet to reach my goals or close my gaps. Based on my goals and gaps, where is the intellectual capital on this campus that I need to be aware of?

Conductor: Well, there's this department over here, there's an office just for that over here, and you need to know Professor Jones is over here.

You: Great, based on where I'm trying to go with my life, where is the social capital on this campus that I need to be aware of? Who are the three to five people that I need to know on this campus that are in your network?

Conductor: You need to know Dean Smith who's over here. He knows all our alumni in your field. You need to know Professor Wilkins who's over here. She can help you get internships. And you need to know Provost James who's over here. She always knows about amazing opportunities for students. There are also two on-campus organizations whose offices are here and here that I think you should consider joining. One of my old students is President of this one, and then another one of my students is Treasurer of this one. Tell them I sent you.

You: Thank you. Finally, is there any financial capital on campus that can help me?

Conductor: Of course, there is the Career Center. That's over here. Talk to Mr. White. Ms. Fields is in the financial aid office, and she knows about all kinds of scholarship opportunities. The Student Activities Office also allows you to apply for funding to start a student organization or put on an event that you think would enrich the campus culture. And this office over here has some money hidden in their budget to send students to national conferences.

Repeat that process with a blank map with at least three additional people. When you put them together, you will have your personalized campus map. UCLA was such a big campus that if you got lost, they would put out an Amber Alert for you. I'm joking, but UCLA was so big that I didn't even go inside every building during my three years there as an undergrad. Every building wasn't relevant to me and my success. What was important was that I knew where the capital that would help me existed so that I could access it and acquire it.

The way we approach college is no different than the way we approach a new cell phone. Since we think we have it all figured out, when we get it, we open the box, turn on the phone to start using it, and we never take a moment to read the manual. Today's phones are more powerful than old NASA mainframe computers that took up the entire floor of a warehouse before Bill Gates introduced the personal computer. Yet, we primarily only use our phones for their top three features—to call, text, and take pictures. If you read the manual that came with your cell phone, you would have a better understanding of what it is capable of, and you would get more out of it. The same goes for college.

When you come to campus as a freshman, you feel small among all these people and buildings. You can't see the forest for the trees. But if you network up, someone with a higher perspective can help you see what you can't and point you in the right direction. You don't have to spend the next four years of time figuring it out on your own. Don't be that senior who is just starting to get it when it's time to go. You can have access to that now if you're willing to say, "I don't know" and ask for help. Stop pretending like you have it all figured out. Admit that you don't know and ask for help.

Exercise 4.1: Campus Tour Conductors

Identify four Undergrad Railroad conductors to conduct this new birds-eye-view campus tour with you using the script above. Also, add why you chose them and use your why statement below when requesting to meet with them for 30 minutes. You may pull people from Exercise 3.3.

Name	Why You Chose Them	Meeting Requested?
	_____ _____	Yes / No
	_____ _____	Yes / No
	_____ _____	Yes / No
	_____ _____	Yes / No

The Process of Expansion Before Elimination

You aren't just in college to get educated, you're here to expand your options. From that expanded awareness, you can choose where you ultimately want to go, and develop a strategy for success. Immediately beginning the process of expansion will allow you to make an informed choice about a major quickly so that you make sure you are on track to graduate on time. Remember that your major likely won't matter unless you are in STEM. One of the greatest causes of delay is when someone chooses a major because they have tunnel vision towards one career path or they are choosing it because other people said it would be good for them. Once on the path, they recognize that it is not a fit for them and they have to change majors which extends their timeline to five or six years and increases the amount of debt they will have upon graduation.

Your first year is about expanding your options, seeing what is available, and understanding who you are and what you want better. Most college students choose their career path based on a limited number of options deemed as good jobs such as teacher, doctor, lawyer, engineer, or businessperson. There is nothing wrong with those career paths, but before committing, you should expand your options first and then begin the process of elimination. If you expand and then eliminate, and end up back on what you originally thought, now you really know that it's a fit rather than guessing and hoping you got it right on your first try.

The number of career paths is not finite — it is infinite. There are new career paths being created right now. Every innovation and evolution leads to new problems which leads to new solutions which leads to new jobs that deliver on that solution. For example, the Uber app alone has resulted in 750,000 new people driving for hire[52]. Don't limit your choices based on who recruits on campus just because it is convenient. Being convenient doesn't mean that it will be a fit. Most companies just see you as a ball of talent that they can mold into whatever they need you to be. When you get an offer letter with 5-figures on it, you feel valued by somebody, and that feels good. What they value is the fact that you followed directions well enough to finish college though they know they will have to train you to do what they need you to do from scratch since most college graduates don't graduate with any real skills or subject mastery.

The quicker you go through the process of expansion, the quicker you can get to the process of elimination and choosing a career path to pursue. Even still, I encourage you to see your first few jobs as paid scholarships to learn real on-the-job skills. You can't teach skills through books and lectures. You don't have to marry your first job. You can date jobs until your early 30s as you seek to find a career that you love.

Since the age of six, we felt we had to have the right answer to the question "What do you want to be when you grow up?" In the first grade, you may have responded with the typical answers such as teacher (because you had one), astronaut (because you saw a moon landing), police officer or firefighter (because you took a field trip), or doctor or lawyer (because your parents thought they were good careers). You didn't really know then, and now you're in college, and you still don't know the answer, but it's okay. The point of this space and time is to discover first and then decide.

Exercise 4.2: A-Z Careers

To show you how limited our scope of possible careers are, I want to play a quick game with you. Set a timer on your phone for two minutes and try to come up with a career path that starts with each letter of the alphabet. Go!

A_____   N_____

B_____   O_____

C_____   P_____

D_____   Q_____

E_____   R_____

F_____   S_____

G_____   T_____

H_____   U_____

I_____   V_____

J_____   W_____

K_____   X_____

L_____   Y_____

M_____   Z_____

Hopefully, you were able to come up with 26 careers. You probably had to get creative for careers starting with letters like X and Y. As you look at the careers you came up with, you'll probably notice that many of them don't require a college degree, yet they still exist. And the career that you ultimately desire may not require a college degree either. Typically, we cut off career possibilities for three reasons:

1. We assume they don't make good money

2. We don't really know what they do on a daily basis

3. We are concerned about other people's perceptions of that career path

Stay open to possibility. I guaranteed that I can find someone who is doing what you love to do and getting paid abundantly for it. It's not a question of "Can I get paid to do this?" The real question is "Do I love it enough to master it so that I can get paid to do it?"

It boggles my mind when someone says they want to be a doctor or a lawyer, but then when I ask them how many doctors or lawyers they have interviewed or shadowed, their answer is none. If you've never interviewed or shadowed someone doing what you think you want to do, how do you know that you really want to do it?

There are people who are doing what you want to do right now. Rather than make huge career choice in the dark based on imperfect information, why not just talk to a few people who are doing the work right now daily. By doing a little more research, you can test if your assumptions and the income potential are true or false. If you think you know what you want to do or be, I encourage conducting at least three informational interviews with people who are doing the work.

Informational interviews are 30-60-minute conversations where you ask someone about the nitty gritty of their work. You ask questions about what they love and don't love, what they wish they would have known beforehand, their hours, their career's impact on their family, trends in their industry, etc. You will gain a better understanding of what they do day-to-day. This information will help you make a more informed decision.

There are three types of careers in what I call The Career Choice Circle:

1. Careers you know exist & know about

2. Careers you know exist but don't know anything about

3. Careers you don't know exist & don't know anything about

The Career Choice Circle

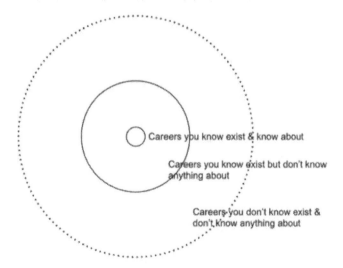

The only career you truly know is one you've done. If you haven't worked somewhere, done an internship, or at least shadowed someone for a few days, then you don't really know what that career is all about. Typically, we romanticize careers based on what we've seen on TV. "I want to be a doctor because I like Scrubs...But I hate blood." The career paths that you know exist and know about are limited because you don't have a lot of experience yet.

There are career paths that you know exist but know you don't know anything about, such as nuclear physicists. I know they exist, but honestly, I don't know what they do every day. I'm certain that smashing atoms together is only a small fraction of what they do though it is the most visible part of their work.

And then there are careers you don't know exist and therefore you don't know anything about. This is the realm you want to expand your awareness of before beginning the process of elimination. Look at the entire menu before choosing what you're going to partake in. Once we have a general endgame in mind, then we can create a strategy to get there. At the end of the day, you must do the research and decide within yourself if and when you are going to allow other people's opinions such as parents, peers, and society at large to determine what you end up doing with your life. Utilize your alumni office to talk to people doing the work you *think* you want to do for a living.

Exercise 4.3: Informational Interviews

List the top three careers that you are interested in and then identify three people you can conduct informational interviews with about that career path. You may have to ask your network up or the alumni office for help. If you want to be a lawyer, find three lawyers to interview. Next, come up with 10 questions you would like to ask during the informational interview to truly understand their day-to-day work.

Top 3 Careers I'm Interested In Exploring	Name of Informational Interview #1	Name of Informational Interview #2	Name of Informational Interview #3

Potential Informational Interview Questions

1. _____

2. _____

3. _____

4. _____

5. _____

6. _____

7. _____

8. _____

9. _____

10. _____

How To Grow Your Personal Capital: Defining Success

There are many ways to grow your personal, intellectual, social, and financial capital while in college. You can find my entire list in my book, *101 Things To Do Before You Graduate*. In this section, I'm going to focus on the number one thing you can do in each form of capital from The Other 4.0 right now to gain momentum.

Remember that personal capital is how well you know yourself. And the primary thing that defines who you are is your personal definition of success. Do you want to be successful? I'm assuming you do. Otherwise, you would not be investing this much time and money into your future. My next question is, have you written down a one-sentence definition of success before? Probably not.

So, you say you want to be successful, but you've never defined it. That's like being in your home driveway, plugging in your home address to Point A on the GPS, plugging nothing into Point B, backing out of the driveway, and driving extremely fast in any direction hoping that one day you'll get where you want to go and assuming you'll know it when you get there. Does that make any sense? No!

It's really important for you to get clear on your personal definition of success because it is driving you and your daily decisions whether you know it or not. Your true definition of success is buried in your subconscious mind and it is playing out even if you say it is something else on the surface with nice sounding words. Until we define success for ourselves, we simply adopt our parents and society's default dashboard of money, power, wealth, fame, and beauty. The truth is, every individual has their own unique definition of success. The challenge is uncovering it among all the programming you've endured since you were born.

You are like a computer. Your hard drive is your body. It carries out whatever the program says to do. Your software is comprised of all the subconscious programs that are installed in you—by yourself but mostly by others initially. These are your underlying beliefs about life, love, money, education, work, success, God, health, etc. And the programmer is you or your conscious mind.

The Reprogramming Process

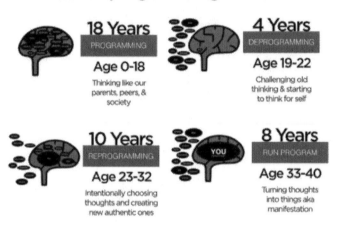

18 Years
PROGRAMMING
Age 0-18
Thinking like our parents, peers, & society

4 Years
DEPROGRAMMING
Age 19-22
Challenging old thinking & starting to think for self

10 Years
REPROGRAMMING
Age 23-32
Intentionally choosing thoughts and creating new authentic ones

8 Years
RUN PROGRAM
Age 33-40
Turning thoughts into things aka manifestation

YOU

From the ages of 0-18, you went through programming. You were programmed by your parents, preachers, teachers, peers, society, celebrities, positive and negative experiences and emotions, TV programs, radio programs, computer programs, summer programs, and youth programs. Up until the age of seven, your conscious mind wasn't strong enough to defend itself from outside influence, and you accepted almost everything as true. The programming continued as you went through formal education and your parents gave your mind over to the school system.

And then from 19-22, your college years, you can go through deprogramming. Deprogramming is the process of uninstalling every program given to you that you are aware of and emptying your mind.

From there, you can challenge, question, release, or re-choose each program for yourself rather than passively accepting what was handed down to you by a member of another generation with a different operating system. The deprogramming stage of life is why so many social movements begin on college campuses. The younger generation is exposed to new thoughts or programs that they hadn't considered before, and they start to question the world and the thinking of the previous generation.

A particular program around diet, God, money, or work may have worked for your parents, but it may not work for you. Just like a computer, old programs don't work as well or at all on new operating systems. Every generation grows up in a different world or operating system. There was a time when the 40-40 Club—working for one company 40 hours per week for 40 years—was the best way to go, but the operating system has changed, and we're now in The Entrepre-New-Reality.

From 23-32, you get the chance to go through reprogramming. Reprogramming is the process of literally making up your own mind. You may re-choose some of the things your parents taught you, but in the areas where you decided to release, you get to create or choose a new belief. For example, you may choose vegetarianism though your parents ate meat regularly. You may choose a different religion or no religion though you were brought up in a particular one. You may choose a more entrepreneurial path instead of trying to climb the corporate ladder. No choice or generation is right or wrong. The choice is either aligned with who you are, or it isn't; to each his own. They chose what was best for them given those times, but times change.

And finally, from 33-40, you can run the program and watch your life unfold based on the pattern of beliefs you have. If, at this point, you are getting what you want out of life and feeling joy, then great. Keep being who you are being and doing what you are doing.

If you're not experiencing the life you desire, then you must go back to the reprogramming or deprogramming stage to identify any buggy programming and then run the program again.

The primary program that runs all our lives is how we define success. You can say success means one thing to you, but deep down inside your subconscious mind you believe something different. You get what you believe, not what you say. Your behavior is revealing what you believe success truly is. So, if you say success is making millions of dollars per year, but your behaviors aren't aligned with that goal, then making millions is not your real definition of success. In this case, one of two things must happen. You either need to change your definition of success to match your behaviors, or you need to change your behaviors to match your definition of success.

When I was in college, I defined success as doing better than my parents. I'm the son of two doctors and come from a lot of privilege. The bar was set high, but I also got to ride the wave of their success. I didn't start where they started. Because my parents were both doctors, many people thought that I was going to be a doctor as well, but that's not what I wanted. I wanted to pave my own path, and I wanted to know that my success was my own, not just me riding my parents coattails.

If my parents got a nice house at the age of 35, I wanted to get one by 30. And if they had a nice car by the age of 25, I wanted one by 20. So, at the age of 18, I bought a 1990 190E Mercedes Benz using money that I saved from working at the batting cage during high school and tutoring during college. I bought it at a used car auction for $3500 and two miles after driving it off the lot it broke down. I ended up spending more money to fix it than I did to buy it.

Two weeks later, my friends and I were in Los Angeles promoting a party we were throwing. I pulled into the parking lot of another party that was happening the night before ours so that we could pass out our flyers. The moment I parked and turned off the engine, two men jumped out of a car in front of me with guns drawn, and I was staring down the barrel of a gun. No words were exchanged. The keys were exchanged, and the car was gone.

The lesson that I learned from that moment was that I was subconsciously living out my parents' definition of success. The only reason I got a Mercedes Benz is because both of my parents had Mercedes Benzes. It was the only car I had ever ridden in my entire life. It didn't make sense for me as an 18-year-old college student with no real significant revenue to have a European car, but it was a subconscious choice. I would have been better off with a Honda Civic.

Oftentimes we subconsciously live out our parents' definition of success, but the real goal is for us to realize that our life is our vehicle to design, drive, and maintain. We have to be in the driver's seat. A lot of people end up backseat driving or Ubering through life while their parents, colleges, employers, and other people are directing their life where they want it to go. To avoid that, you must define success for yourself and how you measure it.

There are two types of success. One type is typically overlooked, but it is, in fact, the most important type. The first type that everyone knows is the destination or where you want to go. This is the point B on the GPS. When success is out there somewhere in the future, it usually means that we feel unsuccessful right here and now in the present. When we say things like "I'll be successful when..." it implies that you're not successful now even though you are planting seeds of success with your daily actions.

The type of success that most people forget about is who you want to be in route to your desired destination. There are many people who get to their desired destination, but they lose themselves along the way. True success is getting where you want to go and becoming the person you want to be while on the journey. But even if you don't reach your desired destination, you want to know at least that you did it your way and had fun along the way. As they say, "The journey is the reward." College graduation only lasts one day. If you didn't enjoy the four years that led up to it, that one day will never make up for the 1460 days that you didn't enjoy.

Exercise 4.4: Your Personal Definition Of Success

Write down a one-sentence definition of success for yourself and three potential ways you can measure it. Be specific. Avoid using vague language like happiness or rich. Imagine what a camera would see when you are feeling successful.

_____

_____

_____

_____

Measurements that will help me know if I'm moving toward success or moments where I will feel successful:

1. _____

2. _____

3. _____

Exercise 4.5: Personal Capital I Need To Acquire Or Develop

Identify parts of yourself that you know you need to develop or improve to create the successful life that you desire and list them below. For example, you may know you need to be less shy and become a better connector and networker.

Add: Things you don't have at all but desire	
More: Things you have and want to increase	
Less: Things you have and want to decrease	
Leave: Things you want to release	

Exercise 4.6: Personal Capital Checklist

Knowing thyself doesn't have to be a vague concept. Here are some things from the *101 Things To Do Before You Graduate* that you can do to grow your personal capital while in college. Check them off, as you complete them, trying to complete as many as you can as quickly as you can. Feel free to create your own. With each one, you will come to know yourself a little bit more.

Self-Discovery

- ☐ Define The Three Ways You Measure Success (Exercise 4.4)

- ☐ Create A Vision Board

- ☐ Take A Personal Development Course

- ☐ Create A "101 List" For Your Life

- ☐ Read *The Alchemist*

- ☐ Visit Your Country Of Cultural Origin

- ☐ Write Your Eulogy (based on what you would want your best friend to say about you)

- ☐ Interview Your Elders (about your family history and build out your family tree)

Personal Assessment

- ☐ Take The Myers Briggs Assessment

- ☐ Take The DISC Assessment

- ☐ Take The Enneagram

- ☐ Take The Gallup StrengthsFinder 2.0

Personal Challenge

- ☐ Read A Spiritual Text From Cover-To-Cover

- ☐ Raise $1000 For A Cause You Care About

- ☐ Journal For 30 Days In A Row (about how you felt you showed up in your life each day)

- ☐ Watch 20 Videos On TED.com or TEDx.com

- [ ] Wear A Costume To Class On A Day That's Not Halloween (to get over worrying what other people think about you)

- [ ] Take An Alternative Spring Break (to challenge yourself)

- [ ] Do Something You'll Likely Get Rejected From Or Fail At (so you can observe how you deal with failure)

- [ ] Volunteer For 30 Hours Per Semester (to uncover how you like to help/serve)

- [ ] Run A Marathon Or Tough Mudder (to challenge yourself mentally and physically)

How To Grow Your Intellectual Capital: The Passion Finder

Once you have a tentative definition of success, another way to develop your personal capital is to get a clear understanding of what your passion truly is and be able to language it succinctly. If you don't know your passion, it won't find you while you're sitting on the couch. You have to be out in the world exploring every interest you have to see if it grows into a passion. Don't be limited by your school's majors. Your passion may have nothing to do with your liberal arts education at all. Yet, you will need to study it and master it during these four years of space and time as if it is your major.

Do you know what Steve Jobs' passion was at your age? It wasn't computers or technology or business. It was calligraphy. If you told your parents you were passionate about calligraphy, how would they respond? Jobs held onto his passion, and that passion for calligraphy, which is the design of language, turned into a passion for design, which ultimately matured into a passion for designing technology, and all of a sudden you have Apple.

Some of you have passions right now that you're ready to give up on because you don't know how you would make a living doing it. There's no major at your school that would allow you to do that passion. And you're worried about what other people will think. Though you may be ready to give up and let it go, I'm inviting you to say, "I'm going to hold onto my passion because I love it and I'm going to continue to develop it because I have no clue how it's going to unfold in the future." If your passion has nothing to do with what you're learning in college, then part of the 24 hours of your 40-hour full-time student work week left over after your 16 hours of classes must be dedicated to mastering your passion.

I'm sure you've heard the advice "follow your passion." That advice skips a key step. Follow your passion and master it so that it becomes a skill that solves a problem for someone else, then the money will follow. The second step is the key. You must find mastery and find a market. Don't let other people's limiting beliefs about themselves—parents, advisors, mentors, friends, family—and what is possible cut you off from pursuing what you love. It's easy to point to this person or that situation to justify why you're doing what you're doing, but that's deflecting responsibility. This is your life. More importantly, don't let your own limiting beliefs cut you off from pursuing what you love.

I want to make a distinction between a passion and an interest. They get used synonymously, but there are levels to this. An interest is a seed of passion but doesn't have the specificity. The more specific you are, the easier it will be to succeed.

Passions have to do with disciplined practice whereas interests have to do with half-hearted play. One of my passions outside of doing this work is playing pool. If you come into a pool hall, you'll see me taking the same shot repeatedly trying to master it. On the next table over, somebody else can be taking a similar shot, but they are just trying to hit the cue ball as hard as possible and pray that something goes in. I'm engaged in disciplined practice, and they're engaged in half-hearted play.

Passions vs. Interests

PASSIONS	INTERESTS
Disciplined Practice	Half-hearted Play
Full-Time (Make Time)	Free Time (If Time)
Action-Oriented	Topic-Based

The other thing about passions is that they are full-time whereas interests are free-time. If you are truly passionate about something, you will make time for it in your day just like sleeping, breathing and eating. You won't stop doing it just because it's midterms or finals week because it is integrated into your life. If you are only interested in something, the moment life gets busy you will stop doing it. You only do it if you have time for it.

The final distinction is that passions are action-oriented whereas interests are topic-based. When you think about your passions, think about them as action verbs in the present subjunctive ending with -*ing*. Interests are like majors—they are a subject or topic, but not a specific action.

Let's say I have a passion for baseball. What career options will allow me to follow that passion? A baseball player is usually the first thing that comes to mind. But on game day, do more than 18 players show up to the field? Yes! Why? Because there's an entire economy around baseball beyond just being a baseball player. You can map out that economy by writing down all the actions that are taking place in the forefront and in the background. Doing so will help you see how money is flowing in different directions within the economy of baseball. Once you know all the actions, it is easier to find a career that's still aligned with the general interest for baseball even if you don't want to be a baseball player or you weren't good enough to be a baseball player.

Here are some examples of action-based passions within the economy of baseball: Hitting baseballs, pitching baseballs, collecting baseball cards, studying baseball history, coaching baseball pitchers, announcing baseball games, managing baseball operations, scouting baseball players. There's a career path connected to every single action I mentioned. Often when we talk about our passion or interest, we talk about them as a topic, but the topic is very general and vague. As you start to think about your passion, I want you to think about it as an action written in the present subjunctive.

I Have A Passion For Baseball

Action Verb		Descriptor
hitting...		
pitching...		
collecting...		cards
studying...	BASEBALL	history
coaching...		pitchers
announcing...		games
managing...		operations
scouting...		players

Let's try another example. Now let's say I have a passion for food. What do you think I want to be professionally? A chef is usually the first thing that comes to mind, but there are many more ways to engage and interact with food than just cooking it. There is growing the food organically, writing food reviews, designing fruit baskets, tasting the food, hosting events around food for the homeless, experimenting with food fusion, hosting food shows, teaching people to cook food healthily. I was watching this cooking show, and the host of the show didn't even know how to cook. She just invited chefs onto her show to teach her viewers. She was still following her passion around food without being the best chef on the planet and enjoying eating the food along the way.

If you went home and told your parents "I'm passionate about designing and fruit baskets," what would they say? They would probably look at you crazy, disown you, and call you a fruit basket. But what does Edible Arrangements do? They design fruit baskets. To be exact, they design $500,000,000 worth of fruit baskets every year. But as a result of caring so much about what other people think, you might give up on your passion when you don't even know what could be possible. Nobody knows. But do you love it enough to try?

Instead of asking "What is my passion?" you can also ask "What problem am I passionate about solving?" Your passion isn't always directly about something you love. It can also be about something you hate. And usually when you hate something you love the opposite. Elon Musk, Founder of Tesla, SolarCity, and Space X is passionate about solving the problem of climate change by changing the way we drive, changing the way we source energy for our homes, and if they both fail, changing where we, as a human species, live. Out of his passion for solving this one problem emerged his various companies.

So if you can't think about what you love, think about what you hate instead. What makes you mad or sad when you see it, hear about it, or experience it? Do you hate how expensive college is? Do you hate unreliable information? Do you hate losing documents on your computer? Do you hate how quickly fashion trends change and trying to keep up? Companies like SoFi, Google, DropBox, and RentTheRunway are solving these exact problems. Your wealth will be determined by the size of the problem you ultimately solve, not your GPA or what school you went to.

I know you want to please your parents. It's innate in all of us. But they cannot live their dreams vicariously through you. Despite my success, my parents still want me to be a doctor to this day. Whenever you decide to pursue a path that is unfamiliar to your parents, a thick layer of fear will emerge because they want you to be safe and secure. As a parent, we believe that our primary responsibility is our child's safety. But beneath that initial layer of fear is an even thicker layer of love. At the end of the day, your parents just want to see you be happy. But the worst thing you can do is spend your life trying to make other people happy while you're unhappy.

Your joy is your job and your parent's joy is their job. And though you love them and want to please them as a way of saying thank you for raising you, this is your life. As a father, I am joyous when my daughter is joyous more than being joyous simply because she does what I want her to do. There may be some difficult conversations to be had, but if someone truly loves you there won't be any conditions and they will want what you want for yourself, not what they think is best for you.

People are getting paid off everything around you. There's somebody who got paid off your shirt, the ink, the marketing, the distribution, the design, the stitching, and the material sourcing. Someone got paid off the light in whatever room you're in from the filament to the manufacturing to the electricity to the installation.

Someone got paid off this book including the printing, shipping, designing, editing, and writing. Money is always floating around you, but it's our limited idea of what's actually possible in terms of a career and a job that's safe and secure that's actually cutting us off from jumping into those income streams and actually doing what we love on a daily basis.

We try to choose a major, and then we try to choose a career that's connected to that major, but the number of career possibilities out there are endless. When I was in your seat, I didn't think of becoming a bestselling author or motivational speaker. Yet today, I make more money doing this than I would have taking a traditional job that they were recruiting for on campus. I don't say this to brag. I say this to say, stay open. If the money were less, my joy would be equal because every day I get to wake up and do what I love which is freeing people mentally, financially, and spiritually. I don't know what the financial prospects are for the path you love and choose, but what matters more than anything is that you are doing what you love daily. That is the goal and true wealth, and four years is more than enough time to find your passion and turn it into a skill that others value.

I have a friend who was interested in archaeology and therefore thought she wanted to be an archaeologist. When you think about the actions that are associated with archaeologist, some passions that may come to mind include digging, discovering, traveling, researching, making connections, and understanding culture. Every profession has passions within it. The real question is what underlying actions are inside the profession that you think you're passionate about? We'll do a personal example together in the upcoming PassionFinder exercise.

Using the profession of Archaeology and its underlying passions, I want to show you a trick. Put the profession aside for right now and just look at the passions. What careers might be good options for this individual given the passions for digging, discovering, traveling, researching, making connections, and understanding culture? Of course, there is archaeologist, but there is also researcher, museum curator, doctor, detective, forensics, and historian. All these career possibilities open up when you start with your passion first.

Often, we are so fixated on the profession that we think we want that we end up limiting ourselves. We put blinders on and can only see with our tunnel vision. My friend ended up being an HR recruiter instead of an archeologist. Instead of digging through piles of rubble, she digs through piles of resumes. Instead of studying ancient cultures, she studies her company's culture to see if college graduates are a fit. She does everything that an archaeologist does, but she's not called an archaeologist.

It's not about the sexy title. It's about your time and whether you're doing what you love daily. Some of us are caught up on the title or getting a Fortune 500 company on our resume, but we don't even know all the Fortune 500 companies. Have you heard of McKesson? In 2018 they were the 6th largest company ahead of Amazon (8th). Have you heard of AmerisourceBergen? They are 12th, ahead of Costco (15th) and Verizon (16th)[53].

The sexiest companies with the biggest brands aren't always the most successful. There are companies on the list that you would just walk by at a career fair because you're so caught up and fixated on the well-known brands and titles. We want those title and brands so that our parents can tell our aunts, uncles and their friends that their daughter is a doctor at this famous hospital or their son is a lawyer at this popular firm or she is a banker at this big-name bank. At the end of the day your title, your salary, and what other people think—including your parents—doesn't matter. What matters most is your inner peace and personal fulfillment.

Throughout my life, I thought I wanted to be a party promoter until my car got stolen. And then I did an internship in Macy's kid's buying department, and I thought I wanted to be in retail. And then through tutoring, I thought I wanted to be a teacher. And then I joined the National Association of Black Accountants, and I thought I wanted to be an accountant. I started testing the waters of entrepreneurship, and I thought I wanted to be Steve Jobs. And at one point, I became a religious zealot and thought I wanted to be a minister.

As of today, I have not done any of those things directly, but through my work, I do a little piece of each of those professions. I don't promote parties, but I host my own live events. I don't market clothes, but I help people market themselves. I'm not a traditional teacher, but I do teach my own courses through TheFreedomSchool.com. I'm not an accountant, but I manage my own business. And I'm not a minister, but I do touch lives every day. Everything that I thought I wanted to be was giving me information about what I would ultimately become.

Instead of getting so attached to the profession, it is more helpful to identify the passion you love doing within the profession. There was a reason you wanted to be a firefighter for a moment. But firefighters do more than just put out fires. Perhaps it was the notion of saving lives that appealed to you. For someone else it may have been the intensity and danger. Find what resonated with you within every career path you've considered without getting attached to the career itself because there are likely other ways to meet that same desire. Locking in on the profession narrows your options. But when you start with the passion first, it expands your career options. Consider the careers you thought you wanted throughout your life and ask yourself, "What is the passion I was actually seeking in that profession?" Doing so will free you from the pressure of deciding right now or acting like you have it all figured out.

Everybody is walking around fronting like they have it together and they don't. Be honest with yourself and be comfortable in the not knowing, the exploration, the adventure, the learning, the seeking, the discovery, the finding. The next time your parents ask you "What do you want to do after graduation?" resist the temptation to give them a profession. Instead say the most powerful three words in the English language, "I don't know." And before they disapprove you can add, "But I do know that I am passionate about this, this, and this, and I'm looking for career opportunities that allow me to do those passions every day. I would love your help finding an opportunity that will allow me to do those things. If you have any friends you can introduce me to, or you come across something, I'm happy to explore it."

This may be a difficult conversation for some of you to have with your parents. But some of the pressure you feel from your parents is not real, it's imagined. It's you thinking they want you to pursue a particular career, but the truth is that they never directly told you that they wanted you to have a certain major and you haven't had a face-to-face sit-down conversation about your future. It may turn out that your parents are not on board with your desires for your life. That's why you need your own personal board of directors—a network up of people who simply want what you want for yourself with no personal agendas or strings attached—to support you in these big decisions. Even with their guidance, the decision always comes back to you.

What word is at the center of your career universe? We just looked at baseball, food, and archaeology. Your word could be chess, bargains, events, people, travel, education, business, or health. In fact, I went to business school with a friend, Erik Allebest, who is really passionate about chess, and he used his time in school to create a multi-million-dollar company at Chess.com. I'm giving you these examples to say that no matter how obscure your passion is, there's a way that you can make a living doing it if you truly love it enough. Once you have your central word, think of all the actions (-*ing* words and phrases) around that central word to map out the economy around it. And then finally, add any descriptors that can help you niche down and get more specific.

Exercise 4.7a: Passion Finder

Use the PassionFinder to map out the action-based economy around your interest and then identify the top passion that you love doing within that economy.

1. Identify your central word or interest (ex. chess, bargains, events, people, travel, education, business, or health)

2. Think of all the actions (-*ing* words and phrases) around that central word

3. Add any descriptors that can help you get more specific

4. Identify the action that you think you are most passionate about doing

Here is an example:

Actions		Descriptors

Exercise 4.7b: Passion Careers And Companies

Based on The PassionFinder exercise, choose the three passions that excite you the most and list them below. Then list careers or companies that might allow you to do that passion on a daily basis. For example, if I was passionate about distributing fashion, I might list fashion distributor or fashion buyer as a potential career and Zara's or RentTheRunway.com as potential companies.

	Careers	Companies
1.		
2.		
3.		

The way to test your passion is to do 30-day experiments. If you've identified several potential passions above, rank the top three in order from most passionate to least passionate. Start with the top one and commit to doing a deep dive into that passion for 30 minutes a day for 30 days. A deep dive means doing it, practicing it, reading about it, learning about it, training in it, or networking around it. If you start with one passion and after four days you fall off, then that is likely not your passion.

Don't get frustrated. Hardly anyone gets it on the first, second, or even tenth try. Get excited that you've crossed something you thought was your passion off your list. That means you are one step closer to discovering your true passion. Move on to the next passion on your list and start the 30-day experiment again. Each attempt is going to give you new information about yourself and your passion. The process will be similar to a heat-seeking missile. You'll get warmer and warmer over time.

Steve Jobs said, "The only way to do great work is to love what you do. If you haven't found it yet, keep searching. Don't settle. As with all matters of the heart, you'll know when you find it." If you go through your top three based on one central word, then try changing your central word, come up with new actions and descriptors, and keep going. Don't stop until you discover it. To dis-cover or un-cover something means that it is already within you, you just have to keep digging, exploring, and experimenting until you find it. Once you find it, it will be easier to identify potential career paths and companies that would allow you to do that passion.

For most of your life, especially with the GPA, you have tried to prove your value by showing to other people like your parents, teachers, colleges, and employers that you can do what the person next to you can do. Look at me, Mom; I can do what my big sister can do. Look at me, teacher; I'm good at physics, too. I'm good at English, too. I'm good at math, too. Look at me, college; my test scores are good, too. I volunteer, too. Admit me. Look at me, employer; I have good grades, too. I'm a student leader, too. Hire me.

Your true value doesn't lie in being able to do what other people can do and being good at a lot of things. Your real value lies within the one thing that you can do that nobody else around you can do. This is why discovering your passion and turning it into a skill will solidify your uniqueness. Many people will have the exact same major as you, but very few people will have your passion.

Exercise 4.8: Intellectual Capital I Need To Acquire Or Develop

Refer back to Exercise 3.2 and choose a subject or skill that you want to master by the time you graduate. This should be a passion or skill that you want to anchor your career around because you believe it will be extremely valuable in 5-10 years. Next, use the 30-Day Learning & Networking Passion Plan below to describe how you will master that subject or skill as if it is your major. For example, you may want to become a better presenter or public speaker, so you go to Toastmasters weekly to develop that skill. To accelerate your process, find other people who share your passion and form a mastermind group that allows you to exchange knowledge and resources as well as hold each other accountable to mastery.

A passion skill I'm committed to developing by graduation:

_____

How do you plan on developing this skill between now and graduation?

LEARNING	
How I can practice by myself	
How I can practice with others	
Books to read	
Websites to follow	

YouTube channels to subscribe to	
Top people to follow who are doing what I want	
Online and in-person teachers and classes	
Companies doing what I want to do	
NETWORKING	
Conferences and events	
Local Meetups	
Student organizations to join	
National organizations to join	
Relevant classes taught here to take	
Faculty and staff who can help	
Departments, Offices & Centers I need to frequent	
Upperclassmen with similar goals	
Friends with similar goals that I can mastermind with	

Exercise 4.9: Intellectual Capital Checklist

Here are some things from the *101 Things To Do Before You Graduate* list that you can do to grow your intellectual capital while in college. You want to develop hard and soft skills. Check them off as you complete them, trying to complete as many as you can as quickly as you can. Feel free to create your own based on your goals and your campus.

Hard Skill Development

- ☐ Master Microsoft Excel & PowerPoint or Apple Numbers & Keynote (or both)

- ☐ Intern With Two Companies

- ☐ Earn A Certificate Or License Relevant To Your Career Path

- ☐ Learn How To Use Photoshop Or iMovie

- ☐ Learn HTML & CSS

- ☐ Get Published

- ☐ Learn A Foreign Language

Soft Skill Development

- ☐ Take A Public Speaking Class

- ☐ Lead A Campus Organization

- ☐ Organize A Huge Event

- ☐ Study Abroad

- ☐ Be A Mentor

How To Grow Your Social Capital

Every success story involves other people. When you look at the world's most successful people, they all move in packs or duos: Bill Gates and Paul Allen, Steve Jobs and Steve Wozniak, Serena Williams and Venus Williams, LeBron James and Dwayne Wade, Candace Parker and the late great Pat Summitt, Jay-Z and Damon Dash, and once those two got divorced, Jay-Z and Beyonce. None of them got where they are alone. Based on their level of self-awareness, they were able to find or attract a partner who was a complement to them.

As someone with a Type-A personality, I found myself by myself, trying to do everything on my own. I was the one who, if there was a group project and my group members weren't doing their part, would end up doing the entire thing, putting everyone's name on it, turning it in, and getting a good grade. I had this mentality of "I'll figure this out. I'll do it on my own. Every man for himself. If it's going to be it's up to me." And of course, there is my favorite one, "Pick yourself up by your own bootstraps." But when you really think about it, someone else had to make the bootstraps. We live in a world of interdependence though we are taught independence. Nobody gives birth to themselves. And very few people know how to grow their own food, build their own house, build a vehicle, start a fire, or sew their own clothes and those are just the basics at the bottom of Maslow's Hierarchy of Needs that we all need. Independence is an illusion unless you can literally feed, house, clothe, and warm yourself.

There is a well-known quote that says, "To go fast go alone, to go far, go together." Doing it by yourself works up to a point, but eventually, it becomes unsustainable. What happens when you don't have the time, skill, or knowledge to complete something by yourself? When I first got to college, I wasn't asking for help, I wasn't going to office hours, I wasn't going to tutoring, I wasn't seeking guidance from my teaching assistants (TAs), and I wasn't getting feedback on my papers. It wasn't until I got a terrible grade on a midterm that I realized I wasn't going to be able to pass that class or graduate without getting help. We perceive asking for help as a sign of weakness, but it's a sign of strength and self-awareness, and asking for help will accelerate you toward any goal you have.

Once you step out of your Do It By Myself mentality and put your ego to the side, you have to figure out who to ask for help. Obviously, there are the people who are paid to help you like professors, tutors, and TAs, but you won't spend most of your time with them. You'll use them for specific help, but most of your time will be spent with your friends. The late great Jim Rohn said, "You are the average of the five people you spend the most time with." Look around yourself right now and ask yourself who you have spent the most time with this semester. Now, who is the smartest in your crew in general? Who is the best at math? Who is the best at writing? Who is the best at science? Who is the best at networking?

If you are the smartest in your crew, two things will likely happen—they're going to end up pulling you down and you're going to struggle trying to pull them up. Everybody you hang with isn't helping you, and you might have to make some changes. Don't try to change them. Instead, change yourself so you can hang with people who are on a higher level and will lift you up.

Your social capital is who you know and who knows you and your friends are a key part of that. I know that you are making friends quickly and hopefully, you've made some great friends so far. But oftentimes a lot of our friendships in college are based on convenience instead of commitment. It's okay for a relationship to start out of convenience, but not to be based on convenience. You'll know if a relationship is based on convenience by who shows up when things get tough.

For example, let's say you started dating someone who lived down the hall. Everything is cool and convenient while you live close to each other. But the moment they move off campus, all of a sudden, the relationship gets difficult. Why? Because the relationship was based on convenience, not true commitment. The same thing can happen in non-romantic relationships. If there is a class that you are struggling with, who is going to show up to teach you what you don't know or encourage you to go get tutoring or invite you to study with them? That's a relationship based on a commitment to your success.

Social vs. Successful Friends

We use the word friend very loosely nowadays. On social media, you accept someone's friend request and suddenly they are a friend. We put them all in the same bucket. "Oh yeah, that's my friend. That's my friend, too—we're roommates. Yeah, that's my friend, I've known her for 10 years. And I just met this person in class this week, but they're both my friends." Everybody is not your friend.

There are two types of friends—your social friends and your successful friends. Your social friends will take you out to a great party whereas your successful friends will take you out of your comfort zone. Your social friendships are based on convenience, and your successful friendships are based on commitment. Your social friends are based on fun and games whereas your successful friends are based on your future and the game of life.

In college, I had two groups of friends. The first group was my social friends. These are the guys that I started throwing parties with during my freshman year. We went to parties together, and we threw parties together. It was great to be engaged in entrepreneurship, but they weren't taking care of business in the classroom. I spent most of my time with them early on, and though I had come into UCLA with some great study habits from the academic rigor of my high school, those started to fade based on who I was hanging out with.

It was the power of proximity and the law of averages at work. If you have 4.0 habits and you end up living with the roommate that has 2.0 habits, what happens? There's a gravitational pull towards 3.0 (= 4+2 divided by 2). It's not exact science, but when you hang with somebody who is on a lower level than you, you will be pulled toward a middle ground like a magnet. You're going to help pull them up, and they're going to help pull you down. That gets magnified when you have 4.0 habits, and you are around three people who have 2.0 habits. That average is 2.5 (= 4+2+2+2 divided by 4). So, you must be intentional about your friend choices.

The second group was my successful friends. I was a business economics major, and they were mostly engineers. Given they were in STEM, the demands of their program were more rigorous than mine. Theirs was the highest of the high in terms of intensity while my major was in the middle of the pack. That made them study more, so if I hung out with them, it would be in a study environment.

I was the only overlap in the two groups. Let's fast forward and look at how their UCLA experiences and my relationships with them played out over time. All my social friends graduated from UCLA late, meaning that they paid 25-50% more for the same piece of paper. Most of my successful friends graduated on time. All my social friends barely finished undergrad while all my successful friends went on to graduate school. I have no connection to my social friends after college. I'm still connected to some of my successful friends today. I don't know where my social friends are in terms of income, but I know for a fact that all my successful friends have six-figure jobs. Who you are surrounding yourself with right now will have a huge impact on the direction of your life. Fortunately, I started spending more time with my successful friends and thus my life reflects more of their lives today.

Social vs. Successful Friends

SOCIAL FRIENDS	SUCCESSFUL FRIENDS
Took me out to great parties	Took me out of my comfort zone
Graduated late	Graduated on time
Barely finished undergrad	Went to graduate school
No connection after college	Still connected years later
5-figure careers	6-figure careers
Still renters	Now homebuyers

Who are your social friends? And who are your successful friends? I am NOT suggesting that you go in your cell phone and start deleting your social friends. Please don't say to someone "You're my social friend." Keep this conversation in your head to yourself. I still want you to know where the party is on Thursday or Friday night. Your social friends are likely good people; they just might not be trying to go where you want to go. And that's okay. Never let your social friends with easier majors determine your social calendar. Just because they can party five nights a week doesn't mean that you can. Go hard with your social friends two nights per week, but study hard with your successful friends five nights per week. Be aware of who you are choosing to spend the majority of your time with.

Here are some things to look for to identify your social friends:

- They sit in the back of the classroom, come late, or don't come at all
- They are on campus, but they never have a backpack with books or a pen to take notes
- They're making social media posts on Twitter, Instagram, Snapchat, every five minutes
- They are always on campus looking fly and spend more time getting dressed than they do focusing on their success
- They don't know where the library is, but they know when and where every party is
- They have a better attendance rate at parties than they do in class
- They are only seeking to finish college, not to win college
- They are afraid to share their GPA
- They don't have a set time and place when they study (e.g., Tuesdays and Thursday from 7:00 pm-10:00 pm in the basement)
- They don't have a wake-up time or bedtime

At this point, you may be realizing that you don't have that many successful friends and some of your best friends are borderline. It is hard to have a friend who is both social and successful. It's binary. They either are, or they aren't. A person who is both social and successful would be someone who parties hard with you on Saturday night until 3:00 am but still wakes you up at 8:00 am on Sunday to go study for your test on Monday. That is a rare individual. If you find someone like that who you can work hard with and play hard with, keep them close.

To attract more successful friends, you must have something to bring to the table. You must be clear about what you bring to the relationship. One-sided relationships don't last. Nobody wants to feel taken advantage of. You have to up your game in a specific area that other people value to create a win-win situation. If you scratch my back in math, I'll scratch your back in physics. Don't just surround yourself with people who think like you either. There is no growth there. Great minds don't think alike. Surround yourself with people who challenge the way you think.

One of the keys to success in college is finding or creating a group of successful friends who are committed to each other's success. You can create a mastermind group that meets regularly to hold each other accountable to academic and non-academic goals. Sometimes formal organizations like pre-professional organizations or fraternities and sororities can serve this function, but they may be too big to create the tight-knit trust circle that a mastermind group requires. In a mastermind, there is no agenda except you are all helping each other get what you want out of college and life. Surround yourself with people who want what you want for yourself with no hidden agendas.

Exercise 4.10: Categorize Your Friends As Social Friends Or Successful Friends

Think about the 10 people you spend the most time with in college right now and categorize them as a social friend or successful friend.

Social Friends	Successful Friends

Exercise 4.11: Social Capital Checklist

Here are some things from the *101 Things To Do Before You Graduate* list that you can do to grow your social capital while in college. The first step is personal branding which pre-determines how you want people to know you and perceive you. From there you can engage in networking and relationship building. Check them off as you complete them, trying to complete as many as you can as quickly as you can. Feel free to create your own based on your goals and your campus.

Personal Branding

- ☐ Start A Blog Or Website

- ☐ Buy Your Own Domain Name (e.g., www.julliengordon.com)

- ☐ Create A Portfolio

- ☐ Clean Up Your Facebook Profile

- ☐ Create A LinkedIn Account
- ☐ Google Yourself & Edit Your Online Image
- ☐ Get Business Cards
- ☐ Get A Personalized Email Address
- ☐ Record A New Voicemail Message
- ☐ Find Two Quality Business Suits

Networking

- ☐ Perfect Your 30-Second Pitch
- ☐ Build A Personal Board of Directors
- ☐ Contact Three Successful Alumni
- ☐ Get A Mentor
- ☐ Start A Mastermind Group With Your Successful Friends
- ☐ Join A National Association Or Organization
- ☐ Attend An Industry Related Meetup
- ☐ Attend A Guest Lecture & Meet The Presenter
- ☐ Join Your Alumni Association
- ☐ Take A Professor To Lunch
- ☐ Conduct Research With A Professor
- ☐ Host A Potluck Dinner
- ☐ Meet The Department Head Of Your Major

How To Grow Your Financial Capital

Earning Money vs. Making Money

Everybody says they want to make money, but very few people study how it works or how it is created. There is a difference between earning money and making money. You earn money through a job in the form of a paycheck while someone else is making it. Making money means creating value by solving a problem for an individual or organization and that money coming directly to you.

Financial literacy is a central part of your liberation arts education. Many of the things you've been taught about money are wrong. Why would you take financial advice from people who don't have the type of money you want to have? That could include your parents, professors, and friends. There are many money myths that keep us from achieving financial freedom faster and here are some that may sound familiar:

- Cash is king.

- Salary is income.

- Save! Save! Save!

- The highest paid person wins.

- Banks are good and protecting your money.

- Student debt is good debt.

You probably believe all of these things, but what if I told you they were the wrong way to wealth. Explaining the truth in detail would require another book, but I'll give you some of the truths right now. Cash is not king. Assets are. Salary is not income. It's revenues. You can't save your way to wealth at a 0.03% interest rate. Using the Rule of 72, it would take you 2400 (72/.03) years at that interest rate to double your money. Banks are bad. They get rid of your money the moment you deposit it by loaning it to other people at over 100-200 times the 0.03% (not 3%) interest rate they are paying you in your savings account. Once you understand money and how it works, it becomes easier to make and multiply.

The best way to understand money is to try to make it. Go and try to sell something and make a profit. Sell lemonade. Sell baked goods. Sell t-shirts. Sell roses for Valentine's Day. Going through the process of buying Dixie cups, lemons, and sugar for $50 and making 100 cups of lemonade that you sell for $2 each will help you understand money, manufacturing, and marketing.

Trying to make a dollar on your own will cause you to appreciate money in a way that earning money somebody else has made cannot. They say "Give a man a fish, and he'll eat for a day. Teach a man how to fish, and he'll eat for a lifetime." A job gives you fish. Seeking to make money teaches you how to fish.

After reading Rich Dad Poor Dad, the information blew my mind so much that I created an unofficial student organization called S.T.O.C.K.S. & B.O.N.D.S. (Sisters Taking Ownership of their Cash and Knowledge of Stocks & Brothers Organizing Networking Dollars and Sense). We didn't go through all the paperwork to get acknowledged as an official group by the school. We were just a mastermind group of students who gathered consistently to learn about financial literacy. We read books like *Rich Dad Poor Dad*, *The Richest Man In Babylon and Think And Grow Rich* together since financial literacy wasn't being taught anywhere else on campus.

It is just assumed that as you earned money, you will automatically know how to manage and multiply it. But that's not true. And it's the reason why 76% of Americans are living paycheck to paycheck despite their education. Even though the United States Census Bureau reports that 32.5 percent of Americans 25 or older have completed a bachelor's degree or higher and 42.3 percent have at least an associate's degree, many college graduates are still financially illiterate.

We also created a business together. We created our own custom weekly planner that we got printed and bound at a local printer. We sold it to students on campus who were dealing with procrastination and made a profit. We also conducted a time management workshop on how to reverse-engineer your syllabi and use the weekly planner to stay on track and avoid pulling all-nighters. I still sell that planner today. It's now called *The Guide To Graduation Student Success Planner* and it has helped thousands of college students manage their time and stay focused on freedom during college.

Sometimes it is faster and easier to package and sell a service than it is to create a product. There is nothing stopping you from creating a dog walking business, a social media marketing agency, a moving company, a pay per pound laundry delivery service, a mobile car wash, a mobile oil change business, a web design business, an Ikea furniture building business, a tutoring business, a photography business, a house sitting or babysitting business, a hair braiding or hair cutting business right now. The startup costs aren't high for any of those. You say you want more money, but are your actions aligned with your words?

Seeking to make money using what we already had within the group was one of the most powerful experiences ever, and we created it ourselves as an unofficial student organization. Starting a business is one of the best ways you can improve your financial capital while in college. Scholarships are great but getting them is out of your control. And a part-time job at minimum wage may cover a bill or two, but it is not going to teach you about wealth or make you wealthy.

There is nothing like the feeling of turning an idea into income. Go sell something. You may not end up creating the next Facebook, but the result of what you create is not the point. The point is that you are grasping the entrepreneurial mindset. Knowing your true value in the marketplace is one the greatest reality checks you can get. It will help you determine what you're doing that matters and what doesn't and cause you to focus on your liberation arts education, not just your liberal arts education.

Avoid Credit Card Debt

Starting a business will help you make money during college, but we also want to make sure that you don't lose any more money than you already are through student loans, the interest, and forgone wages. The next biggest culprit is credit card debt. Credit card debt and student loans are cousins born from the same predatory uncle. In 2016, over 30% of active students had an average credit card balance of $2,573[54]. Now, fifty percent (50%) of college students have four
or more credit cards, and 30% of students had "maxed out" their credit cards.

There is a reason why freshmen look better than upperclassmen. It's not because they have yet to add on the Freshman 15. It's because they don't know how to manage money and they end up swiping and spending for things they don't need but think they deserve now that they are an adult.

What typically ends up happening to freshmen is that they burn through their refund and any monies they get from their parents then find themselves in a precarious situation. But they are too embarrassed to ask for help because even with all that algebra and calculus, they still don't know how to manage money. As the end of the semester approaches, the questions become "How do I pay my car note? How do I pay my cell phone bill? How do I eat?" This is why Top Ramen is known as the breakfast, lunch, and dinner of broke college students. After spending all your money, credit cards look like a savior. Where the credit card companies get you is in the fine print and "hidden" fees such as annual fees, balance transfer fees, cash advance fees, finance charges, over-the-limit fees, and late fees.

The Journey Student Card from Capital One has a $0 annual fee but a 24.99% variable APR. This card's interest rate is 833 times higher than your 0.03% savings account APR. This is called usury and arbitrage. I encourage you to look up the definition of these words yourself. Essentially, financial institutions are giving you a low return when you have excess cash and charging you lots more for the same cash when you are in extreme need. Misuse of a credit card can negatively affect your credit score which sticks with you and can cost you thousands of dollars as I'll show you in a moment.

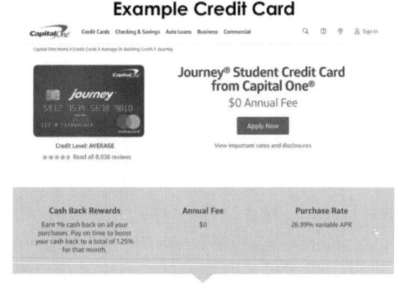

Example Credit Card

Image Source[55]

How does your credit score work? According to Equifax, in general, "the longer you allow a bill to go unpaid, the more damaging the effect it has on your credit score. For example, all other things being equal, a payment that is 90 days late can have a more significant negative impact on your credit score than a payment that is 30 days late. In addition, the more recent the late payment, the more negative of an impact it could have." If you miss a payment (even just one) on one of your credit accounts, the late payment could remain on your credit report for up to seven years[56].

Additionally, "one late payment could have a more significant impact on higher credit scores. According to FICO data, a 30-day delinquency could cause as much as a 90- to 110-point drop on a FICO Score of 780 for a consumer who has never missed a payment on any credit account.

In comparison, a consumer with a 680 FICO Score and two late payments (a 90-day delinquency on a credit card account from two years ago and a 30-day delinquency on an auto loan from a year ago) would experience a 60- to 80-point drop after being hit with another 30-day delinquency[57]."

Debt is the result of seeking to reap faster than you've sown. Colleges, companies, and creditors prey on 18-year-olds. These clowns would show up at your 18th birthday with applications and a "card" if they could. The moment you officially become an adult, credit card companies will be setting up tents on your campus to try to get you. The credit card companies give out "free" t-shirts that say the word "COLLEGE" on it or small football helmets with your university's logo on it to entice you to join them. It only costs them $3 for those souvenirs, and they are happy to give them to you because they intend to make $3,000 off your spending.

Go to https://www.freecreditreport.com and get your credit report to make sure it is accurate and that there are no creditors reporting things that shouldn't be there. You should be starting with a clean slate. Your score won't be high because you haven't proven that you can handle credit yet. The average credit score for someone 18 to 24 years old is 630, according to Credit Karma, and that's not great[58]. Though it is 630 out of 850, a 630 score will not get you the best mortgage rates, an auto loan with a 0% interest rate, or the lowest auto insurance premiums. In some cases, it won't allow you even to rent an apartment without a cosigner.

Everybody loves extra credit. Well, I have some for you. But it's not on a test. It's for your credit score. Next, you have to understand compound interest and how it works for you and against you. Einstein said "Compound interest is the eighth wonder of the world. He who understands it earns it; he who doesn't pays it." Again, the people charging you interest do not have your best interest in mind. A 4% interest rate doesn't sound high right? You imagine that if you spend $100, you will only have to pay $4 in interest. If you borrow $1,000, you would only have to pay $40 in interest. If you borrow $10,000, you would only have to pay $400 interest. That could be true, but it really depends on the repayment terms. The math isn't as straightforward as you think.

You can use this website to assess any type of repayment or amortization schedule:

https://www.bankrate.com/calculators/mortgages/amortization-calculator.aspx

You need to know the principal which is how much you borrowed, the interest rate and whether it is fixed or variable, the term or years the agreement is for, and how often you are required to make payment (e.g., monthly).

Given this, $10,000 at 4% for one year is not $400 in interest. If you make 12 monthly on-time payments of $851.50, you will only end up paying $217.99 in interest. But what if you spent that $10,000 to get a car or pay for tuition as a student without a salaried job or consistent income? You likely won't have $851.50 per month to pay it back because working for minimum wage at the library isn't going to yield that monthly. So, what happens is that term gets extended until there is a payment that is manageable for you. You may feel grateful for "lower payments" but "lower payments" equals more interest over time. If we take that same $10,000 at 4% and extend it out over five years, your monthly payments are only $184.17, but you end up paying $1,049.91 in interest rather than $217.99. That's a 382% increase.

An extra $100 in interest here and there may not feel that bad, but that is not where your credit starts to hurt and get out of hand. Small dings on your credit score occur when you miss a payment and are late. You have a chance of "ish" happening and missing one of 60 payments over 5 years than you do of missing one of 12 payments over a year. Those dings decrease your credit score and end up affecting your interest rate for big-ticket purchases like a car or a home years later. Your credit score represents your trustworthiness to pay back debt on time. And if you don't demonstrate that you can pay back $100 on time regardless of what your age was, what you were going through in life, or what financial literacy you had at that time, then why would a creditor trust you with a $15,000 loan for a car or $300,000 mortgage for a house? The lender would mitigate its risks by increasing your interest rate.

Let's see how a few dings on your credit report can impact you over several years. Say you wanted to get a $100 pair of shoes and it was the end of the semester, so you were out of money, but you had a credit card. You think to yourself, "I can make $10 payments for the next twelve months and pay this off." So instead of buying them with $100 cash because you didn't have it, you put it on your credit at a 15% interest rate for a year. A payment of $8.31 seems small right?

Extra Credit

$100 at 15% for 1 yr
DIFFERENCE OF $8.31

$100

+ $8.31 = $108.31 + late fees
+ $415.41 = $423.72
+ $64,158.83 = $64,582.55

$15K at 5% for 5 yrs, interest = $1,984.11
$15K at 6% for 5 yrs, interest = $2,399.52
DIFFERENCE OF $415.41

$300K at 4% for 30 yrs, interest = $215,608.52
$300K at 5% for 30 yrs, interest = $279,767.35
DIFFERENCE OF $64,158.83

But during those 12 months, you move twice just like a normal college student. You move out of your dorm in May, home for summer, and then back to a new dorm in the Fall. Why is that important? Because your credit card statements were being sent to your old address, therefore you missed them and forgot to make your payment though you were earning money from your summer job. Now you miss one payment, and then you miss another payment, and then you miss a third payment because you didn't automate your payments from the beginning and your account is 90 days delinquent. You end up getting late fees plus a ding on your credit report. The late fees hurt now, but the ding on your credit score won't affect you until you apply for credit again later.

Let's fast forward three years after misusing that credit card at the end of your freshman year. You've graduated from college on time, and now you want to get a fairly new Honda Civic with low mileage that costs $15,000. You and your jalopy are both 22 years old. You made it through college together, and it's time to let it go.

But when they run your credit for the certified pre-owned car, they see this ding on your credit report. So, instead of getting the car loan at 5% for five years which would have cost you $1,984.11 in interest, you are now getting it at 6%—just 1% difference—and the interest will cost you $2,399.52 all because of those shoes that you didn't pay back on time that you needed so badly for that party to impress people who are no longer in your life today.

The creditor thinks to themselves, "You haven't proven that you could pay $100 back on time so why am I going to give you $15,000 without covering my butt? I'm going to cover my butt by charging you a little more interest because this is riskier for me." So, you end up paying $415.41 more in interest because of that 1% difference in your interest rate. So, now those shoes actually cost you $100 in principal, plus $8.31 in interest on the shoes, plus $415.41 in additional interest on the car for a total of $523.70. That doesn't even account for any late fees on the missed shoe payments.

But wait a second. It's not over. Now you see that beautiful house that you really want, and people are making offers on it right now and your best offer will require $300,000 dollars. You apply for a mortgage at the bank. If you had good credit, you would have received that mortgage at 4%, but because of that ding on your credit report from those shoes from years ago, the bank is only willing to give you a 5% interest rate. At 4%, you would have paid $215,608.52 in interest over 30 years. But because of those shoes, at 5% you'll now be paying $279,767.35. That's a $64,158.83 difference due to the 1% difference in your interest rate. So, now those shoes that you really wanted from freshman year have actually cost you $64,582.55 plus late payments. That's an expensive pair of shoes. Depending on what school you go to, that could be 2-3 years of tuition and housing.

The twisted thing about credit is that you need to use it to gain it. I hate to write this, but based on how credit works, you have to go into debt to gain access to more debt. It is like when you first learned how to swim. At first, you started in the 3-foot kiddie pool, and once you proved to your parents that you could handle that, they let you go into deeper and deeper water. Regardless of how deep you are eventually allowed to go, you're still underwater. When you hear someone say a mortgage is underwater, it means, the market value of a home today is lower than the current balance owed on its mortgage. In other words, you are drowning in debt.

Therefore, if you have a credit card, I encourage you to keep it. Don't close it. Ironically, closing cards can hurt your score because it reduces how much credit you have access to. The fact that you have a card means that you've officially started building your credit history and part of your score is based on how long you've had credit. Don't close it but cut it up or put it in a cup of water and then freeze it. You don't need to keep credit cards in your purse or your wallet. They aren't for daily use. Out of sight, out of mind.

Choose your lowest single monthly payment and automate the monthly payment to build your credit. An easy one to automate is your cell phone bill. It's something that is monthly, hopefully not a lot of money, and that you always pay. Automate your credit card to pay your cell phone bill and then automate your checking account to pay that credit card off monthly. That will build your credit score and history over time. Do this one thing and then hide the credit card from yourself. You do not want to add credit card debt on top of your student loans. Credit cards can really hurt you after you've made mistakes. And then when you need credit for big-ticket purchases that you need to finance later like a car or a home, creditors gouge you.

Here are some examples of credit cards offered to students so that you can see the typical APR.

Credit Card Offers

Image Source[59]

Exercise 4.12: Financial Capital Checklist

There are some key things that college students must know and do regarding their finances to improve their financial position during this time. Check off as many of these things from the *101 Things To Do Before You Graduate* as you can below and do the work necessary to check off the ones you haven't completed yet.

Managing Money

- ☐ Open A Checking Account

- ☐ Open A Savings Account

- ☐ Complete Your Monthly Budget Or Cash Flow Statement (from Exercise 3.5)

- ☐ Complete Your Balance Sheet (from Exercise 3.4)

- ☐ Save A $1,000 Emergency Fund

Credit

- ☐ Get Your Free Credit Report

- ☐ Get A Credit Card (and take a picture of the front and back and then cut it up or freeze it)

- ☐ Automate Your Credit Card To Pay Your Monthly Cell Phone Bill (and then automate your checking account to pay your monthly credit card bill)

Making Money

- ☐ Buy And Read *Rich Dad, Poor Dad* by Robert Kiyosaki

- ☐ Buy $100 Worth of Stock In The Company You Spend The Most Money With (besides your college) using the Acorn or Robinhood app or your bank

- ☐ Sell All Your Old Textbooks Online At The End Of Each Semester

- ☐ Try To Sell Something And Make A Profit (e.g., lemonade, t-shirts, flowers, etc.)

- ☐ Write A Business Plan

- ☐ Get Your Real Estate License

- ☐ Apply For At Least One Scholarship

Job Hunting

- ☐ Create And Edit Your Resume

- ☐ Post Your Resume On Three Job Boards

- ☐ Do A Mock Interview

- ☐ Conduct Three Informational Interviews With Professionals About Career Trajectory And Salary

- ☐ Know Your Answers To The Top 20 Interview Questions

- ☐ Prepare Five Unique Questions For Every Interview

- ☐ Get Three References Or Recommendations

- ☐ Meet With A Career Advisor Each Semester

- ☐ Do Company Research

- ☐ Attend At Least Two Career Fairs

- ☐ Recruit A Career Team

- ☐ Read A New Industry-Related Article Every Day For 30 Days

PRIORITIZE

How Do I Prioritize Everything?

You didn't come to college to stay the same. The only difference for many graduates is that they are four years older and have 5-to-6 figures worth of debt. You came here to grow your Other 4.0 and develop yourself. When people say you graduated college, they are using the wrong definition of the word graduate. There are two definitions of the word graduate:

1. successfully complete an academic degree, course of training, or high school (as in "I graduated from college")

2. arrange in a series or according to a scale (as in "a graduated cylinder")

The second definition, however, is more appropriate. We know that when you graduate from college, nothing magical happens. The doors of opportunity don't fly open because you've acquired a 10-cent piece of paper. Graduation is not the goal. For your graduation day, relatives are going to fly in from all over the country to come see you. It is going to be a celebratory day of hugs, smiles, flowers, food, and cards. But little do they know that when they fly out the next day, on Monday morning you have no place to go in terms of work.

College graduation is a ritual, but it doesn't signify a real result except that you were able to complete a certain amount of credits while maintaining a minimum required GPA. In other words, you know how to go to school, read and skim books, write papers, and take tests good enough. Even if you truly mastered the information taught in your major, information changes quickly in the information age, therefore, that's only temporary success. The only type of education they can't take away from you is self-mastery because that will last a lifetime.

In high school, you may remember using a graduated cylinder for an in-class chemistry experiment to measure the volume of liquid. A measuring cup used for cooking at home is also graduated which you can see based on the lines and numbers on the outside of the cup. In a graduated cylinder, each line represents a degree and degrees are a unit of measurement. **The truth about college is that graduation is not a one-day event. You graduate—or not—every single day. You're not in college to get a degree—you're here to graduate yourself by as many degrees as you possibly can.** Each day you are making hundreds if not thousands of choices that graduate, upgrade, up-level your life, and increase your degrees of freedom—or not.

What are degrees of freedom? A degree of freedom is no different than a black belt in karate for fighting. While holding a black belt is a very impressive accomplishment, it does not mean that one has reached the upper echelons of karate skills. Once a person tests into the black belt rank, there are still 10 levels that must be accomplished before the final belt can be earned. You may have heard the term 6th-degree black belt or 9th-degree black belt. The way college is set up, everyone gets a black cap and gown, but in truth, there are levels to this. There are degrees with a degree.

Below are examples of degrees of freedom in terms of financial freedom, mental freedom, and time freedom. They are all yes or no questions. Either you have these degrees of freedom, or you don't.

Degrees of Financial Freedom

- I have the freedom to make money while I'm asleep
- I have the freedom to make money without exchanging significant amounts of time
- I have the freedom to make money on demand
- I have the freedom to give to family and friends without any expectation
- I have the freedom to donate joyously to causes I care about
- I have the freedom of having no bad debt that I have to pay for (student loans, consumer debt, single family home)
- I have the freedom to order what I truly want rather than ordering on a menu from right to left (price to meal)
- I have no material wants
- I have the freedom to quit my job if I want
- I have the freedom of knowing that no single person or company can derail my life tomorrow
- I have the freedom created by passive streams of income

- I have the freedom of having 2, 3, 4, 5, 6, 7 streams of income
- I have the freedom of knowing I have a 3-month, 6-month, 1-year emergency fund
- I have the freedom to buy anything I want under $300, $600, $1,000 without worrying
- I have the freedom to earn as much as I would like
- I have the freedom of only having good debt that pays for itself (e.g., cash-flowing rental property or business)
- I have the freedom of having assets that generate passive or semi-passive income which covers 50% or 100% of my living expenses (a.k.a. what I really need to survive)
- I have the freedom of having assets that generate passive or semi-passive income which covers 50% or 100% of my loving expenses (a.k.a. what I really want to thrive)
- I have the freedom of investing in stocks without worrying about a 20% loss
- I have the freedom to invest
- I have the freedom to command over $100 per hour for my skills and time

Degrees of Mental Freedom

- I am in perfect health
- I feel worry-free
- I feel free to love with all my heart
- I feel free to say what I want to say
- I feel free to go where I want to go
- I feel free to practice my religion

- I feel free to believe what I truly believe openly and speak my truth
- I feel free to express sexuality in a way that is true to me
- I feel free to look how I want to look (e.g., dye my hair, wear whatever I want)
- I have the freedom to observe my emotions and consciously choose the most helpful ones in the moment
- I have the freedom to be myself without fear of judgment
- I have the freedom to celebrate the success of others without comparing or getting jealous knowing there is more than enough
- I have the freedom to pursue my purpose in faith
- I have the freedom to know when a thought is authentic to me and when it is not and choose with that awareness
- I have the freedom to release expectations of others and accept who they are and how things are right now
- I have the freedom to be present in the moment versus being too past or too future oriented
- I have the freedom to be open to new ideas without feeling wrong or like I have to defend mine
- I have the freedom of knowing that it is not just me by myself—that I have people in my corner who will help me if I fall or fail

Degrees of Time Freedom

- I have the freedom to start my workday when I want
- I have the freedom to create my own schedule (e.g., early

bird, night owl, 9:00 am – 3:00 pm)

- I have the freedom to work on what I want

- I have the freedom to work with who I want on my team

- I have the freedom to work with who I want as clients

- I have the freedom to work where I want (e.g., office, home, abroad, the beach)

- I have the freedom to work in whatever clothes I want

- I have the freedom to work as few hours as I want

- I have the freedom to take as many days off as I would like

- I have the freedom to take 2, 4, 6, 10, 16 weeks of vacation

- I have the freedom to stop working for a day without asking permission or worrying about money

- I have the freedom to not work for 3 days, 5 days, 2 weeks, a month, 3 months, a year, or at all

- I have the freedom to say no to clients

- I have the freedom to take naps during the traditional work week

- I have the freedom to choose how I spend the first 15 minutes of my morning

- I have the freedom to love at least 80% of what I do weekly (4 out of 7 days per week)

- I have the freedom to not work on weeknights and weekends

- I have the freedom to delegate, outsource, or automate tasks

I don't love doing

· I have the freedom to volunteer for causes I care about

These are just some degrees of freedom in terms of financial, mental, and time freedom. At this stage of your life, you have bought a lot of time freedom so that you can create more financial, mental, and time freedom afterwards. If you don't use this time properly, this will be the last time you have freedom for a while—perhaps until the mid-life crisis or retirement. Only you can write your ticket to freedom. A college diploma will not do it for you. The goal of your time in college is to increase your degrees of freedom.

The real hard choices in college are not just the big ones like your major and career path. The real hard choices are the daily choices between your best self and base self that will either decrease or increase your degrees of freedom. **The more base self choices you make, the more basic your life will be. The more best self choices you make daily, the greater the chances of you living your best life.** Again, it is binary. Base self or best self? Base self or best self? Base self or best self? There are thousands of forks in the road every day. And once you learn to see them, you can consciously choose. With every choice you are creating your future whether you know it or not. The only thing valuable I learned from Shakespeare was "To be or not to be." I'll add "To do or not to do. That is the question."

Here are some daily *graduation-based* choices you make between your best self and your base self.

· Do I go to class? Do I not go to class?

· Do I sit in front? Do I not sit in front?

· Do I ask that question? Do I not ask that question?

· Do I go to office hours? Do I not go to office hours?

- Do I make those flashcards? Do I not make those flashcards?

- Do I get my paper edited by The Writing Center? Do I not get my paper edited by The Writing Center?

- Do I go to tutoring? Do I not go to tutoring?

- Do I read the chapter? Do I not read the chapter?

- Do I do a second draft? Do I not do a second draft?

- Do I ask for help from that smart guy or girl in my class? Do I not ask for help from that smart guy or girl in my class?

Here are some daily *growth-based* choices you make between your best self and your base self.

- Do I exercise? Do I not exercise?

- Do I eat a healthy breakfast? Do I not eat a healthy breakfast?

- Do I listen to an inspirational or educational podcast during my commute? Do I not listen to an inspirational or educational podcast during my commute?

- Do I read that self-help book? Do I not read that self-help book?

- Do I apply for that scholarship? Do I not apply for that scholarship?

- Do I meet the head of my major? Do I not meet the head of my major?

- Do I take that unpaid internship? Do I not take that unpaid internship?

- Do I meet that alumni? Do I not meet that alumni?

- Do I stay late to hear that guest speaker? Do I not stay late to hear that guest speaker?

- Do I volunteer? Do I not volunteer?

- Do I run for that leadership position? Do I not run for that leadership position?

- Do I take that online skills-based class connected to my passion? Do I not take that online skills-based class connected to my passion?

- Do I apply for that summer internship? Do I not apply for that summer internship?

- Do I start saving to study abroad? Do I not start saving to study abroad?

- Do I go to that networking event? Do I not go to that networking event?

The choices are binary. Like the degrees of freedom, they are yay or nay, yes or no. The choices are always between your base self and your best self. Your base self is your lower self. It is the small you. It is the part of you that is drawn to staying the same, not because it is better, but because it is familiar and comfortable. It looks and feels easier to follow your base self in the moment, but following your base self makes your life harder later. Whenever you choose it, you lose. Your best self is your higher self. This is what higher education is supposed to be about. Your best self is the bigger you. It's the part of you that is drawn toward growth. Whenever you choose it, you win in the moment and in the long-run.

You reading this book right now is a win in comparison to other people who are sleeping, playing video games, watching Netflix, scrolling through social media, or stressing because of an assignment that is irrelevant in the larger scope of things. You won't choose your best self every time, and that's okay. I want you to enjoy this experience, and your base self will create some great memories that you can laugh at until the day you die. But more importantly, your best self will lead you to a life you enjoy versus sporadic moments here and there.

Achieving success just requires some foresight and the ability to delay gratification. In this on-demand Amazon Prime economy, we want what we want now, but the most meaningful and valuable things take time, consistency, and focused energy to develop. In order to change the momentum, you must win the small decision first like do I drink water or soda, do I wake up at 6:00 am or hit snooze, do I sit in front or in the back. Winning those small battles helps you ultimately win the war inside.

College gives you four years of time to develop yourself. That's what makes it unique. The question becomes "What would you do with four years of space and time if your life depended on it?" If I gave you a scholarship that covered all your basic living expenses for up to four years, how would you invest that time? You don't have to go to college. You could do whatever you want with these four years. However, you know that whatever you do during that time will send your life on a trajectory of success, keep your life the same, or send your life downwards. What are some things you would do in that four years of space and time to send your life on a trajectory of success?

Most people have difficulty answering this question because up until this point of their lives, they have waited for other people to tell them what to do next to grow themselves. They waited for guidance from their parents, counselors, preachers, or teachers instead of looking inside themselves and listening to their intuition. As a result, when you finally have the freedom and opportunity to choose for yourself, you feel helpless. **Your intuition is your inner guide. And it is the cheapest form of tuition there is.** Do what it tells you and take the tests it pushes you towards, and you'll be in good shape. You've relied so much on other people's voices that you may not be able to hear your own, but it is still there. If the path to success was a paved road that others could point you down, then surely more people would be successful. In order to achieve success, you will have to follow your intuition and best self to pave your own road.

This is a rare four years of space and time and how you use it will shape the trajectory of your life. It's like bowling. If you're off track early, you'll end up in the gutter. But if you're on track early, you have the potential to strike big in life. Since becoming a teenager, you've desired more and more freedom. Now, with the autonomy to create the life of your dreams, do you know what to do with it without anyone telling you to enroll in these classes, take this test, go to this school, apply for this job, or join this organization? College is a four-year stepping stone to your 40-year career. And during that four years, every day you are either winning the day or losing it.

I've said it before, "It doesn't matter what school you go to. What matters is how you go to school." In addition to how you show up to classes (which only makes up 40% of the college experience), your relationship and approach to grades, your "free" time, work, student groups, friendships, relationships, fun, and sleep also affect you because they will make up the rest of your college experience. You are extremely smart and talented, so amazing opportunities will always come to you. The question is how do you prioritize them? Given that, I'm going to walk through several success strategies that distinguish the way a successful student navigates college versus an unsuccessful student.

Two Students. One Campus.

	Unsuccessful	Successful
Classes	Schedules them according to what's available & friends	Schedules them according to time they learn best & professors
Grades	Tries to get As in all classes	Sets grade goals. Doesn't try to be great in everything. Knows what's enough.
Gaps	Has no intention for gaps	Intentional about gaps at the beginning of the day
Involvement	Tries to be involved in many orgs	Deep involvement in a few orgs
Studying	Tries to do it all on their own	Forms study groups, goes to office hours, and gets tutoring
Homework	Tries to be perfect	Knows what good enough is
Work	Works as many hours as they can to try to get "rich"	Works just enough based on their budget and uses the other time to get involved
Friends	Lets friends with easier majors determine social calendar	Declares when he or she is going to have fun in advance and says "No!"
Sleep	Sleeps anytime there is a gap	Sleeps strategically (e.g. timed naps)

Strategy #1: Class Choices

How you choose classes can have a big impact on your success in college. We already discussed how most students didn't do the proper research when they chose the college they attend. That unconscious movement also guides how many students choose their major and individual classes. Unsuccessful students schedule classes according to what's available and what their friends are taking. Successful students schedule classes according to the time they learn best and the professor teaching it.

I'm an early bird so I used to love morning classes and would intentionally choose them. After the second week of classes, those who are night owls would stop attending, and as a result, their grades would suffer, and that shifted the grading curve in my favor. It sounds simple, but if you're not a morning person, don't choose morning classes. It will be hard to uproot 18 years of programming in one semester. There is nothing wrong with being a night owl if your most important activities are based in the afternoon and night.

Enrollment periods for classes can be tight. If your enrollment window opens at 12:01 am then you need to be up at that time to get the classes you desire. If a class you really want isn't available, get on the waitlist, show up on the first day of class, introduce yourself to the professor, and explain why you need this class now. Show them your 4-Year Academic Plan from Exercise 1.2 and how this class fits into it. Students who are enrolled will drop, and if there are enough seats, exceptions can be made.

The best way to research classes is to talk to upperclassmen in the same major as you. There are also sites like RateMyProfessor.com, but a first-hand account from someone who isn't bitter just because they got a bad grade is a better basis to decide upon. For high demand classes or larger general education classes, there are usually two or more professors who teach it, and usually one is better than the other. By better, I mean that the professor is able to teach the material better and demonstrates a deeper passion for teaching than the other professors. Just because someone is smart in a subject—which is why schools hire professors —doesn't mean they can teach it or even desire to teach it. **The way a professor shows up will impact how you show up, so you want to identify the best professor for a specific class, which semester they teach the class, and adjust your 4-Year Academic Plan accordingly.**

Choose classes based on your learning style and strengths. Just because you got into the same college as someone else doesn't mean the playing field is suddenly level. All K-12 systems are not created equal. Your K-12 experience may not have been a college-preparatory environment. Now that you're in college doesn't mean that you're automatically ready to succeed. Many first-year students' professors are disgruntled that their students can't write a solid paragraph. It's usually not the students' fault. For a K-12 system to have a student's mind 18,720 hours over the course of 13 years and the student still not be able to write isn't the student's fault.

The challenge for that student is to manage their classes while intentionally getting support on developing that skill; otherwise it will haunt them throughout their undergraduate experience. The foundational skills needed to succeed include reading, writing, grammar, basic math, studying, note-taking, time management, and money management. These are not a given just because you're an adult now. And you typically don't realize how ahead or behind you are in these basic skills until you compare your notes to someone else's or you read a friend's paper and see the difference between the quality of their writing, grammar, and thinking and yours.

Strategy #2: Grade Goals

Some people think they are failures because they have measured their self-worth by their GPA. Your GPA is not a reflection of your worth or your smarts. There is a reason you didn't get an A in that class, and it wasn't that you couldn't do it. When you're honest with yourself, you know that you didn't care, and you didn't see the relevance. But rather than deceiving yourself that you are going to get an A in every class, why not just declare your goal from the beginning. If you want to go to graduate school, then you'll need a strong GPA, but it doesn't have to be a 4.0. Though it seems counterintuitive, unsuccessful students start each semester with the goal of getting As in every class while successful students set grade goals. Successful students choose which classes they want As in and set minimum grade goals for classes they don't care about and know are irrelevant.

I graduated from UCLA with a strategic 3.3. I didn't have a 4.0. My 3.3 wasn't because I was taking it easy. It was the exact opposite. I had a 3.3 because I was taking advantage of all the opportunities that I could on and off campus that would help me to win college, not just finish college. Though important, the world's most successful people didn't have the best GPAs. There are other measurements that correlate with your long-term success better than the GPA alone, like The Other 4.0.

When I applied to Stanford, the most selective business school in the world, there were people who had perfect GMAT scores and perfect 4.0 undergraduate GPAs who didn't get in, and I did because of what I did with the rest of my time during college outside of the classroom. That's what set me apart. I could have gotten a 4.0 in college if I really wanted to, but I would have had to focus 100% of my energy on classes, and that would have caused me to miss out on the real richness of college that takes place outside of the classroom.

The strategic GPA is happening consciously or unconsciously. Why not just be honest about it from the beginning of the semester. Setting grade goals relieves you of the stress of trying to be a jack-of-all-trades and the disappointment of not being one no matter how hard you try. The poster child of most schools is the valedictorian All-American athlete with a perfect 4.0. While that is great, that is not the goal. Don't compare yourself to archetypes and unrealistic standards. **It's not about being the smartest—it's about being the most strategic.**

Each semester, choose the classes you want to master and get As in. This should be at least half of your classes. I used the A-A-A-B-B-C grade goal strategy. That's three As, two Bs, and one C grade. If you do the math based on grade points earned, that's 4+4+4+3+3+2 which equals 20. Twenty grade points divided by 6 classes equals a 3.33 or B+ average.

To identify the class that you want to get an A in, ask yourself:

1. Which classes am I excited about?

2. Which classes are essential to get into or complete my major?

3. Which classes speak to my strengths (e.g., paper-based, project-based, test-based, homework-based)?

4. Which classes are easy and can boost my GPA?

To identify the classes that you don't need to get an A in, ask yourself:

1. Which classes am I dreading because they are known to be hard, or I wasn't academically prepared for during K-12?

2. Which classes are required but irrelevant to my future?

3. Which classes grade based on my weakness?

4. Which classes do I just need to pass?

People have different strengths and learning styles, and some classes and majors play to some people's innate strengths and learning styles. Lectures may or may not work for you. You may be a more visual learner. You may love to write or not. You may be better at presenting your ideas verbally than putting them to paper. All this information about yourself should help determine which classes you choose. There will be required classes that go against the way you learn and what you desire to learn and that's okay. Those are the classes that you set a realistic grade goal in, get tutoring, and go to office hours for support. If you set a grade goal of a B and you get a B+, then great. You will feel better and less stressed than striving to get an A and still getting a B+.

Exercise 5.1: Set Your Grade Goals For This Semester

Set your grade goals for the semester based on the classes you chose, how prepared you feel, and how much you care about each subject.

Class	Grade Goal	Grade Points	Actual Grade	Grade Points
Math 101	B+	3.33	A-	3.67
	Strategic GPA		Actual GPA	

Grade Points:

A = 4.0	A- = 3.67	B+ = 3.33	B = 3.0	B- = 2.67
C+ = 2.33	C = 2.0	C- = 1.67	D+ = 1.33	D = 1.0
D- = 0.67	F+ = 0.33	F = 0.0		

Strategy #3: Reverse-Engineer Syllabi

Syllabi aren't new for students. In K-12, you probably got a syllabus with some classroom rules and a supply list that your parents had to sign. In college, the syllabi are 10-pages long and include the rules, grading rubric, every assignment, and due dates. Unsuccessful students live by the seat of their syllabi. They wake up every day and wing it. Successful students reverse-engineer their syllabi into their time management system to a point where they don't even need to look at their syllabi anymore because everything has been broken down and mapped out into micro-assignments.

In high school, your teacher probably reminded you about your homework assignments every single day. It was likely written in the upper left-hand corner of the chalkboard daily. They were essentially breaking down larger assignments into micro-assignments for you just like a parent breaks down a child's food so that they can consume it. In college, your homework is buried in dense paragraphs of your syllabi, and it is up to you to extract the daily micro-assignments you need to be doing to complete the larger assignments on your own. Unfortunately, nobody teaches you this. It is assumed that you'll just figure it out. This is a tedious process. It will take about 1-2 hours per class at the beginning of each semester, but it will make your life easier and your grades higher.

I'm going to walk you through the steps to reverse-engineer your syllabi. This process helped me graduate from UCLA in three years. It took a full day at the beginning of each academic term, but it saved me so much time and worry throughout the quarter. Taking one day of time to shave off a year of college and save $25,000 was well worth it to me. Ultimately, you want to break up all your assignments into micro-assignments. Micro-assignments are any action that requires your brain to switch tasks (e.g., researching to critical thinking to writing to editing) and takes 15 or more minutes. For instance, if we were writing a three-page paper, coming up with a thesis, reading the book, writing the first draft, writing the bibliography, and editing the paper would all be individual micro-assignments because they require switching your thought processes and each action takes longer than 15 minutes.

Exercise 5.2: Reverse-Engineer Your Syllabi One Paragraph At A Time

Let's start with one paragraph within a syllabus I found online. Read the assignment below and see how many micro-assignments you can identify. Also, estimate the time you think it will take to complete each micro-assignment.

Part 1 - First Draft of Resume and Cover Letter (25 pts.):

An important goal of this course is for you to leave with a polished and professional resume, as well as an understanding of the role that resumes and cover letters play in the job search process. As such, this is a two-part assignment:

1. Resume and Cover Letter: Search online for a job that interests you. (If you don't know where to start looking, try Jaguar Jobs, monster.com, and careerbuilder.com). Once you find a job that piques your interest, create your resume and a targeted cover letter for that position.

2. Individual Critique/Career Coaching Session: Sign up for a time to meet with a career advisor from our Career Services office. During the meeting, you will review your resume and cover letter and discuss where you are currently in your career exploration process and individual professional development.

Part 2 - Final Resume and Cover Letter (25 pts.):

Based off the feedback you received during your individual meeting with a career advisor, create a polished copy of your resume and cover letter (again, target to a specific job).

I noticed _____ micro-assignments and they include:

	Micro-Assignments	Estimated Time (Min)
1		
2		
3		
4		
5		
6		
7		
8		
9		
10		
	TOTAL TIME (HOURS):	

Given the micro-assignments listed above and the sequencing, this assignment will take _____ hours, and I should start _____ days before it is due.

I noticed seven micro-assignments and they include: find a job you like (60 minutes), write first draft of resume (60 minutes), write first draft of cover letter (60 minutes), meet with coach (45 minutes), write final draft of resume (30 minutes), write final draft of cover letter (30 minutes), and have an extra meeting with coach for review (45 minutes). This assignment will take approximately 5.5 hours. And you can't start it the night before because it requires you to meet with your coach which means that you need to schedule that appointment in advance. Overall, this assignment will take at least three days to complete if your coach is readily available.

These micro-assignments are what you put onto your Weekly To Do List and Weekly Time Grid in *The Guide To Graduation*. So, if the assignment was due on September 30th and you wanted five days to complete it, you would place the first one or two micro-assignments on September 25th, the next one or two on the 26th, and so on. Now imagine doing this for every major paper, project, reading, and test in your syllabi. It will take time, but your entire semester will be mapped out. You'll know when things are going to be heavy and you'll never get behind. Writing a paper, reading a book, or studying for a test will never sneak up on you because you reverse-engineered, not only your syllabi, but your success.

Once you do this, you'll immediately experience the simplicity, ease, and freedom it adds to your college experience. It will free you to take advantage of the richness of college that occurs outside of the classroom. While college offers you a ton of freedom, true freedom requires structure. It's no fun being at a party when you know you have a 10-page paper that you haven't started yet due at 8:00 am the next day. You want to have guilt-free fun. This one action will put you light years ahead of everyone else who is still waking up and winging it with their syllabi.

Strategy #4: No Free Time

If I followed two students during the first week of school, I would know who is going to be successful versus who is going to struggle based on what they do in the gaps in their schedule. The gaps in one's schedule is where students fall through the cracks. By gaps, I mean the large blocks of time between your classes.

Unsuccessful students believe in the idea of free time in college. Successful students are fully aware that college has a cost per minute (see Exercise 1.6) and they are always seeking to get a return on their investment . What are you doing in the gaps in your schedule which I call your "freedom time?" Attending class for 12-16 hours is easy. Anybody can show up and sit in a seat. Just because the professor has your time doesn't mean they have your attention. You may be there physically, but it doesn't mean you're there mentally. You don't get as many attendance points in college as you did in high school. Your success will be determined by what you do outside of class in the same way that an athlete's success will be determined more by what they do in practice or the gaps in between their games such as their conditioning, skill development, rest, and study.

There is no such thing as free time in college. Full-time student is your full-time job. **Assuming that you only have 16 hours of class per week and sleep 7 hours per night, you have 103 hours per week to allocate. That is not "free time." It is your time to get free or your "freedom time."** This is not vacation. It's the pathway to your vocation. Before you leave for class every day, you should have crystal clear intentions for how you are going to use the gaps in your schedule. You should know that once your first class ends at 11:00 am, you are going straight to the library to knock out that 90-minute problem set, and then you're taking a 30-minute lunch break before heading back to the library to write the first half of your 10-page paper due in three days. This is what it looks like to be intentional about the gaps in your schedule from 9:00 am to 5:00 pm just like a job.

The most dangerous days are the days where you don't have classes. You may have a Tuesday - Thursday schedule or a Monday - Wednesday - Friday schedule. The days you don't have class may be perceived as days off or extended weekends. That is not the case. Every day you should be seeking to grow at least one of your four capitals which will ultimately determine your degrees of freedom with your freedom time. Ask yourself, "What do I need to do today to manage my classes? And what can I do today to lead my life?"

Strategy #5: Strategic Sleep

It is true. Naps are the secret to happiness. Preschoolers have it figured out. In fact, preschool was probably the last time you had a nap in the context of school. The difference between naps in preschool and naps in college is that there was someone there to wake you up in preschool and it was timed. In college, it's all up to you. It's a nap when the intention is to re-energize yourself so that you can wake up and do something productive. It is plain sleep and sometimes depression when you go to sleep just because you can.

The way we are trained to go to school from 8:00 am - 3:00 pm and work from 9:00 am - 5:00 pm goes against our bodies natural ultradian rhythm. The ultradian rhythm is your body's natural cycle that is present in your sleeping and waking life, and it oscillates about every 90-120 minutes. Power naps are a way of leveraging your natural ultradian rhythm to your advantage.

There are a few simple criteria for an effective power nap.

1. Set the intention to re-energize for a specific activity once you awake

2. Set an alarm to wake you up

3. Sleep for no longer than 90 minutes

4. Time the nap to start when you normally feel a dip in your energy

Your success in college isn't just about time management—it is also predicated on energy and sleep management. Yes. I'm encouraging you to go to sleep during the day, but do it strategically with intention. Your body needs a certain amount of rest to perform optimally and it will correct any sleep deficit you create by any means necessary even if that means making you sick to get you to slow down.

When you look at the world's best athletes, they are just as strategic about their rest as they are about their activity. Most games have frequent breaks whether it's the end of the quarter, half-time, timeouts, commercial breaks, or pauses in between plays. These are opportunities for physical and mental rejuvenation. In fact, fitness is defined as the speed of recovery. The more fit you are, the faster you recover.

Your game is learning. It is mainly mental. Though your brain only takes up 2% of your body mass, it uses up 20% of your energy. Conscious thought drains you quickly. This is why cramming tires you. You think you're just going to cram for six hours before the test, but you barely make it to two hours without yawning because of your ultradian rhythm. This is why you need a sleep strategy.

People make it seem like the harder you work, the less sleep you should be getting. But it's the opposite. The harder you work, the more rest you need to recover so that you can do it again. If you don't get the appropriate rest to account for your previous activity or your upcoming activity, you will burn out. Did you know that Michael Jordan took naps before games? Rest is how you stay physically and mentally sharp. Your brain needs its own half-time. Cutting your day in half with a nap will prevent you from starting your day with high energy and then just getting lower and lower and lower throughout the day until you crash and burn.

With a midday nap, you start high, dip a little bit, nap, start high again in the early afternoon, and then dip a little until your bedtime. Though you are not a little kid anymore, sticking to a specific bedtime is critical to your sleep strategy. It dictates when you will wake up and how much energy you will have throughout the day ahead. If you execute this simple strategy of sticking to a bedtime plus a strategic nap, you will never get as low as the person who tries to stay up for 16-20 hours per day. Your higher energy levels when you are awake will lead to higher productivity and learning. In addition to that, you will likely have more hours awake per day. A one-hour nap could break up one long 16-hour day into two 9-hour days for a total of 18 productive hours versus 16 depreciating hours. If you know that you won't go back to campus and get involved, then don't go home to sleep. Find your nook in the basement of the library or some other place that is free of distractions so that you can get some shut eye and then wake up and focus again.

Strategy #6: Leadership Over Membership

When students hear catch phrases like "Get involved!" and "Have new experiences!" some take that to mean, join as many student organizations as you can. While you should explore all of the organizations tabling on Org Day and see which groups interest you the most, ultimately, you should only fully commit to one or two. You don't want to get spread too thin. If you do, meetings and commitments will start to overlap, and the organization you value the most implicitly will win out while the other ones fall off anyway.

Having lots of student organizations and activities on your resume may make it look longer, but it doesn't speak to the quality of your experiences, only the quantity of them. You want to seek leadership over membership. Being a member doesn't say much about you unless there are strict membership requirements that make the group exclusive. You can be a member, pay dues, and never show up. Membership is a passive act and doesn't tell an employer anything about what you're capable of doing. Anybody can be a member —membership doesn't mean or show anything.

Leadership demonstrates true commitment. Whether you are the president or just a committee member, you are a leader committed to moving this organization and its membership forward. You are responsible for some sort of metric or initiative that allows you to test, practice, and discover your skills. When you step into the role of leadership, others naturally start watching you—not just when you're in front of the podium, but at all times. Knowing that will challenge you to be on your A-game often. I'm not saying you can't turn up at a party. Humans love people who are real, authentic, and not just one-sided. Just know that you are in the public eye and stay consistent. Know that wherever you go, you are representing yourself and your organization.

Leadership experience is something you can talk about and be proud of. What can a member talk about? I attended some meetings and went to their big gala. There is no value demonstrated in that. It's passive versus proactive. Leadership is one of the most valuable skill sets in today's economy, and college is a safe-to-fail environment where you can test out your leadership skills and take risks in a way where nobody gets hurt if you mess up. Companies want to know that you know how to navigate uncertainty, can move the needle on something you deliberately set out to achieve, and know how to influence other people toward a common goal. A good GPA shows that you know how to take care of yourself. Leadership shows that you know how to take care of other people.

You don't have to be the president of the student body government or even an official student organization. You could lead a fundraiser for a cause you care about. You could lead a campus referendum to change a policy that affects students. You could lead the day shift team at the campus eatery. You could lead a committee in a fraternity, sorority, or student organization. You could lead an intramural sports team or the league. You could lead the cheers at the football and basketball games. You could lead a free hugs campaign. You could lead a blood, toy, food, or coat drive. You could lead a Spring Break study trip. You could lead an alumni mentorship program. You could lead a business pitch competition. There are many more ways to lead on-campus and off-campus. I just want to get your brain churning so that you can start to see the traditional and non-traditional leadership opportunities all around you. Envisioning something that you want to see on or off campus that doesn't currently exist or you think can be better and getting other people involved in creating it with you is leadership.

Strategy #7: Don't Work For Money

Don't work for money. The American Dream won't tell you this, but real wealthy people work as little as they have to for money. The Puritan work ethic tells you to work harder and longer than the next person, and you'll be successful. But if the hardest worker always won, then day laborers would be the most successful people in this country. **The hardest worker doesn't always win, but the winner does work hard. Hard work is one of several essential ingredients to success.**

If anything, work for experiences, not for money. Outside of class, you want to dedicate as much of your time towards enriching experiences, skills, relationships, and mentorship that will pay you in ways that a one-digit per hour job can't. An unpaid internship that helps you develop your personal, intellectual and social capital is more valuable than a minimum wage on or off-campus job that gives you $10/hour. Let's be clear that your part-time job in college is not where your upside is. That's not what's going to make you rich. Look for a great boss to work under or a great business to work in, not just a job.

The cost of college has leaped six-fold since the 1980s. With state budget cuts and parents contributing less, the burden falls on the full-time student. A new survey from Citigroup and Seventeen magazine finds that almost 80% of students take at least a part-time job during the school year[60]. The survey calculated that on average, these students work 19 hours a week. According to 2015 research done by the Georgetown University Center on Education and the Workforce (Georgetown Center), about 40% of undergraduates work at least 30 hours a week and 25% of all working learners are simultaneously employed full-time and enrolled in college full-time[61].

I'm not suggesting that you should not work. In fact, gaining work experience puts you ahead of the pack. But it has to be the right type of work experience. Serving at Applebee's isn't going to serve you well on your resume unless you intend to own an Applebee's or go into the restaurant industry. And working at the library won't help you much unless you plan to become a librarian. On top of that, most work-study and part-time jobs for college students pay the minimum wage or close to it. Even a student working full-time at the federal minimum wage of $7.25 per hour would only earn $15,080 annually, which would not cover tuition and living expenses at most colleges. The upside comes from how you maximize this four-year period in your life to pole vault you, your existing family, your future family, and your finances into another social strata.

Therefore, you must spend your time growing your personal, intellectual, and social capital so that you can convert what you've developed into financial capital later. **A minimum wage job will always be there. This four-year opportunity won't be. You want to work as little as possible for money in college.** So how much should you work? You should only work to supply what you need. After you get your financial aid package and they deduct tuition, housing, and healthcare, you will be left with your refund check. That refund check is supposed to support you for the entire 16-week semester or 10-week quarter and should be budgeted accordingly.

Let's say your refund check is $1600 and is supposed to last you

16 weeks. That's $100 per week. But when you do your budget which includes your cell phone, car note for a newer car or maintenance on an older car, insurance, gas, parking, fun, and eating out, it comes out to $200 per week. You have a $100 weekly deficit. So, you need a job that will cover that gap weekly. The federal minimum wage is $7.25, so you would simply do the math to determine how many hours per week you should work. But make sure you don't forget to account for taxes—a 10% federal tax and another 1-5% state tax—on whatever you earn.

Here's how you do the calculation if the federal tax rate is 10% and your state's tax rate is 5% for a total of 15%:

$$\text{The Maximum Hours I Need To Work Per Week} = \frac{\text{Monthly Expenses} - (\text{Refund} / \# \text{ of Weeks in Term})}{\text{Hourly Wage} \times (1 - (\text{Federal Tax Rate} + \text{State Tax Rate}))}$$

$$\$100 / (\$7.25 \times (1-(10\%+5\%)))$$

$$= 16.2 \text{ hours per week}$$

Here it is in words. You work for 16.2 hours at $7.25 per hour and earn $117. The state and federal government take 15% of your check off the top and leave you with $100. You use that $100 to fill the gap in your budget.

Go here to find your state's tax brackets:

https://taxfoundation.org/state-individual-income-tax-rates-brackets-2018/

Federal Tax Brackets

Single

Taxable Income	Tax Rate
$0 – $9,525	10% of taxable income
$9,526 – $38,700	$952.50 plus 12% of the amount over $9,525
$38,701 – $82,500	$4,453.50 plus 22% of the amount over $38,700
$82,501 – $157,500	$14,089.50 plus 24% of the amount over $82,500
$157,501 – $200,000	$32,089.50 plus 32% of the amount over $157,500
$200,001 – $500,000	$45,689.50 plus 35% of the amount over $200,000
$500,001 or more	$150,689.50 plus 37% of the amount over $500,000

Married Filing Jointly or Qualifying Widow(er)

Taxable Income	Tax Rate
$0 – $19,050	10% of taxable income
$19,051 – $77,400	$1,905 plus 12% of the amount over $19,050
$77,401 – $165,000	$8,907 plus 22% of the amount over $77,400
$165,001 – $315,000	$28,179 plus 24% of the amount over $165,000
$315,001 – $400,000	$64,179 plus 32% of the amount over $315,000
$400,001 – $600,000	$91,379 plus 35% of the amount over $400,000
$600,001 or more	$161,379 plus 37% of the amount over $600,000

Married Filing Separately

Taxable Income	Tax Rate
$0 – $9,525	10% of taxable income
$9,526 – $38,700	$952.50 plus 12% of the amount over $9,525
$38,701 – $82,500	$4,453.50 plus 22% of the amount over $38,700
$82,501 – $197,500	$14,089.50 plus 24% of the amount over $82,500
$157,501 – $200,000	$32,089.50 plus 32% of the amount over $157,500
$200,001 – $300,000	$45,689.50 plus 35% of the amount over $200,000
$300,001 or more	$80,689.50 plus 37% of the amount over $300,000

Image Source[62]

If you can get a higher paying job, then you obviously can work less. Then there are also other jobs on campus that can offset certain expenses. For example, becoming a Resident Advisor will likely provide you with free housing and food in exchange for your leadership and time.

Exercise 5.3: Calculate How Much You Need To Work

Since the goal is to work as little as possible for money, identify exactly how many hours you must work per week to meet your monthly expenses so that you can focus the rest of your time—your freedom time—on taking full advantage of the college experience.

		Example	Yours
Deficit (if any) from the monthly budget you created in Exercise 3.5	A	$400	
Divide that number by 4 weeks in a month	B	$100	
Enter your hourly rate or find the minimum wage for your state here https://paywizard.org/salary/minimum-wage	C	$7.25	
Use the 10% federal tax bracket in the chart above unless you plan to make more.	D	10%	
Get your state tax bracket from this website https://www.tax-brackets.org/	E	5%	
Calculate the maximum amount of hours you need to work per week to meet your monthly expenses = B / (C x (1-(D+E))	F	16.2 hours	

EXECUTE

How Do I Get Everything Done?

There are 168 hours in a week. If we deduct weekends, which is two days or 48 hours, and then we deduct sleep, which is seven hours per night, you are left with 85 (= 168-48-7x5) hours of waking weekday hours to allocate. Earlier, it was said that 40% of undergraduates work 30 hours per week, so that brings us down to 55 hours to allocate.

So, let's assume that you have 12 credits this semester and each credit is an hour of class. That's only 12 hours of class per week bringing our total down to 43 hours. That may be a Monday, Wednesday, Friday schedule where you're in class four hours per day or a Tuesday, Thursday schedule where you're in class six hours per day. However it is broken down, class is not a majority of your work though you're supposedly a full-time student.

In addition to classes, there are homework assignments, reading, writing, and projects, but most students don't have scheduled time for that. Instead, they procrastinate until an assignment is due. Therefore, they experience heavy weeks throughout the semester, like midterms week, instead of breaking things up into micro-assignments and doing parts of them daily throughout each week. If a student treated their study times like a class where it was permanently scheduled throughout the week, they wouldn't have the heavy weeks that lead to high stress, sickness, and less sleep.

Supposedly, for every one-credit hour in which you enroll, you will spend approximately two to three hours outside of class studying. According to the Bureau of Labor and Statistics, full-time students only spend 3.5 hours on educational activities outside of class[63], and a bulk of that is cramming around test times. So let's use two for now. That's an additional 24 hours of study if you have 12 credits. So now you're down to 19 hours to allocate toward your growth and development outside of fulfilling your commitments for school and sleep.

How Average Students Spend Their "Freedom Time"

Time use on an average weekday for full-time university and college students

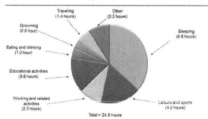

Image Source[63]

So, what should you do with the rest of your time—your freedom time? Every single hour you have left should be dedicated to creating the life you want after college and liberation arts. This is where your self-directed curriculum comes in. You should look forward to your freedom time and seek to maximize it by minimizing the things that are unimportant and irrelevant in the larger scheme of your life. Beyond your major, what are you seeking to master? If your major doesn't matter, how are you going to differentiate yourself from the nearly 4 million other graduates with equal or better degrees from equal or better institutions with equal or better GPAs than you[64]? This unstructured time in your schedule is when your base self and best self go to war, and you determine who wins. This is an inner battle, not an outward one. You may blame your college, your professors, your K-12 education, your job, your parents, your financial aid office, etcetera, but at the end of the day, it call comes back to you.

How To Avoid Pulling All-Nighters

Being strategic about your GPA and your gaps is the key to success in college and requires an effective time management system. Every time management system has three components. The first component is your calendar or your vision. This lays out what you want to do and by when. You can use Google Calendar, Microsoft Outlook, or a paper calendar like the one inside *The Guide To Graduation*. Your monthly calendar will include your major assignments, tests, quizzes, papers and project due dates, big events, and other deadlines. Next is your To Do list, your strategy, which lays out what you have to do to complete or get ready for the things on your calendar. Your To Do list should be weekly. This is where you put all your homework assignments, things to study, readings, and micro-assignments that you reverse-engineer from your syllabi.

And finally, there is your Weekly Time Grid. This lays out how you will invest your time to complete your To Do list items.

Exercise 6.1: Weekly Time Management Process

Because of my time management system, I graduated from UCLA in three years without ever pulling an all-nighter. The prerequisite for this to work is that you reverse-engineered your syllabi already. Here is my step-by-step process for planning out my week in advance for 20 minutes on Sunday night or Monday morning:

1. Get a blank To Do List and Weekly Time Grid here:

   http://www.undergradrailroad.com/planner

2. Open your Monthly Calendar (e.g., Google, Outlook) to see what is coming up this week and next week that you need to start now.

3. Add any new personal and academic things to your To Do List that need to get done this week. Your To Do List should already have items on it based on the reverse-engineering of your syllabi at the beginning of the semester.

4. On your Weekly Time Grid, fill in or scratch out the times that are already scheduled such as classes, meetings, travel (e.g., by car, bike, bus, train, and foot), meals, naps, sleep, fun time, getting ready for the day (e.g., shower, brush hair and teeth), and winding down at night (e.g., shower, chill).

5. Calculate the available hours or gaps you have that are unscheduled each day.

6. Now one-by-one, anchor each item on your To Do List into a gap in your schedule as if it is a doctor or dentist appointment until they all have a time slot.

7. Any gaps left over on your Time Grid after these steps are your real freedom time to pursue your liberation arts education.

The goal of this process is not to make you so busy that you feel burned out. Its goal is to give you an accurate picture of the week ahead so that you know exactly what you need to be doing in the gaps in your schedule which nobody else will hold you accountable to but you. This is how you stay on track without stress or pulling all-nighters.

Planning Your Week

	1. Calendar = Vision		2. To Do List = Strategy		3. Time Grid = Plan
	What do I want to achieve? By when?		What do I have to do to achieve it?		How should I invest my time accordingly?

Is College Worth It?

Here's the truth: If you want to have different, then you need to be and do different right now. However, the truth won't set you free; acting on the truth will. If you want to be an entrepreneur, start creating a company now or go work for free for an entrepreneur you admire. If you want to be a doctor, go volunteer at the hospital. If you want to be in TV or radio, go intern at the college TV or radio station. If you want to own real estate beyond your own home, take a real estate investment class. If you want to be a writer or journalist, then write a book or articles for the school newspaper. If you want to learn how to speak Chinese, then study abroad in China. If you want to be a teacher, then master a subject you love whether it is your major or not and teach as a Teacher's Assistant, tutor students who need help, or teach on YouTube.

Is college worth it? My answer is yes, yes, yes, yes, yes. Despite how much you're paying, I still believe college is worth it, but your major may not matter so make sure you get a masters in yourself. This time is about self-mastery and discovering who you truly are and what you truly want. Succeed in the classroom but fail as much as you can outside of it. Try new things and take risks. Expose yourself and expand your options before engaging in the process of elimination. You are buying experiences not just an education. If you want an education, go to YouTube University or Wikipedia for free. What Wikipedia, YouTube, and just about any online university can't give you are the experiences and community that your college offers. Information can be handed to you through the internet. Experience can't—an experience must be had. And this is an investment in your dream not the guarantee of a job. I wish I could guarantee you the job of your dreams at graduation that paid you abundantly, but that's not the economy that we're in today. We live in The Entrepre-New-Reality where you must know your worth and be able to prove it beyond a reasonable doubt.

I'm going to leave you with this story. Growing up I had a dog named Buddy and Buddy's yard was surrounded by this red fence on three sides and the other side was the wall of the house with my bedroom window. We never took Buddy out for a walk because his yard was big enough to do everything that he wanted to do. One day, on a Sunday, my dad came downstairs and said, "Do you want to take Buddy for a walk?" I said "Okay!" We go in the garage, find the leash in a box, and put it on Buddy. Buddy starts panting with his tongue out and jumping on his hind legs in excitement. We open the red gate from the top lock and take Buddy for a walk. Instead of us walking Buddy, Buddy walks us. The leash is fully extended for 30 minutes up the hill and back.

When we got back, we put Buddy back in the yard, took off the leash, and let him go. The next day, on Monday, we went off to work and school. When we got home that evening, Buddy was gone. Buddy dug a hole under the fence and escaped. Fortunately, our neighbor caught him, saw his dog collar, and realized he was ours. When he saw our car in the driveway, he brought him back. My dad plugged up all the holes under the fence with rocks, and we put Buddy back in the yard. On Tuesday, we went off to work and school again. And when we came back home that evening, Buddy was gone again. There were no holes under the fence. The only way Buddy could have escaped this time was by jumping off the top of the dog house over the fence. This time Buddy never came back.

Until this day I do not know if Buddy is alive, but what I do know is that Buddy lived. Once Buddy saw what was on the other side of that red fence, he realized how small he was living and he couldn't stay in that small little area anymore. It was enough when all he knew was what was inside the red area, but once he saw what was on the outside, he realized that he couldn't stay there anymore.

In our own lives, we all have red fences. Those red fences are our own limiting beliefs about what's possible for our lives. My hope is that this book has opened you up to new possibilities beyond your red fences so that your red fence disintegrates, and you experience more possibility than you could have even imagined at this moment

217

in your life. Buddy taught me that it's not until you push something to its perceived limits that it realizes that it is limitless.

You have two paths before you—the easy road or pave your own road, your base self or your best self, finishing college or winning college, liberal arts or liberation arts, bondage or freedom. **Graduation day is only a one-day event, but graduating yourself is a daily process.** At the end of it all, the only degree that matters is your degree of freedom. I conquered college and used it to free myself. But the feeling I have every time I go to speak on a campus knowing that thousands of students are being swindled instead of being strategic is best described by the words of my inspiration, Harriet Tubman, when she crossed the Mason-Dixon Line on September 17th, 1849:

> *"I had crossed the line. I was free; but there was*
> *no one to welcome me to the land of freedom.*
> *I was a stranger in a strange land; and my home*
> *after all, was down in Maryland; because my*
> *father, my mother, my brothers, and sisters, and*
> *friends were there. But I was free, and they should*
> *be free also. I would make a home for them in the*
> *North, and the Lord helping me, I would bring*
> *them all there."*

Go forward!

Your conductor on The Undergrad Railroad,

Jullien Gordon

THE AFTERWORD

For High School Students

If you're in high school, college is on the horizon. Everyone is saying go though they aren't pulling out their checkbooks and you may still feel unsure. Knowing why is important. Going because you're "supposed to" go isn't enough. Start planning your escape route now to see if college is actually the best path to get where you want to go. Knowing what I know now, if I was still in high school with the intention to go to college and win college, here is what I would do step-by-step.

1. **Enroll In A Community College:** Instead of going to a 4-year institution, I would go to the closest decent community

college to complete my general education requirements with the intention of transferring to a prestigious 4-year institution. Unless, of course, at the 4-year college you have scholarship funds that reduce your out-of-pocket and/or loan amounts to the same or equal cost of attending the community college. Community colleges tend to have low graduation rates (38% overall completion, and a 47% drop-out rate), so you will have to stay focused and disciplined if you take this route[65]. Never forget the long-term game and be mindful not to surround yourself with people who don't have the same intentions and ambitions as you. If you play your cards right and get your General Education requirements done for a fraction of the cost, you can save five figures on tuition for years one and two.

2. **Join The Honors Program:** Most community colleges have an honors program, and those in the honors program get an experience equivalent to that of a traditional 4-year college, if not better. Each program has its own criteria so research the 10 closest community colleges to you and find out what the admission criteria are. Ask about the transfer rate and success of their last class of students and see if they can put you in touch with someone who ended up transferring to the school you hope to get your bachelor's degree from.

3. **Live At Home:** Instead of living on-campus, I would recommend living at home. I know that many students see college as a chance to escape home, but I'm trying to help you escape debt. Your dorm room is likely going to be smaller than your bedroom at home, and you won't have any privacy their either. At least at home you might have your own bedroom. The downside is that you will likely have to commute instead of being able to roll out of bed and walk to

class in your pajamas. If you live at home, you can save a ton on housing. Two more years isn't going to kill you, but the debt accrued by not living at home when you don't have a full-time job to afford the true cost of living *will*. You will miss out on the on-campus housing experience during your first two years, but there are students who live on-campus and still don't take advantage of those opportunities. Their path is just class to dorm and dorm to class although the real richness of college is in the spaces between class and dorm. You'll make friends with people who live on campus and can arrange to stay on campus with them when you want or need to. Rather than rushing home right after classes finish, make a commitment to stay on campus until 7:00 pm daily whether you're studying for your liberal arts education or advancing your liberation arts education.

4. **Scholarships:** Top-tier schools are looking for talent. But you have to dominate academically for this to work. Keep in mind that your competition will be less steep at the community college level. Make sure you rise to the occasion rather than dropping down to the crowd. Some people don't apply for scholarships because they believe they are too privileged, and others don't apply because they feel they aren't good enough. You won't know if you don't apply. We are eager to write essays to get into college or for a grade in college, so why not continue writing them to get money to pay for college. Like the college application process, many of the questions on various applications will be similar and simply need minor tweaking to fit what the selection committee is looking for in a quality candidate. You may be able to transfer to a top-tier school fully funded.

5. **Transfer To A Flagship 4-Year College:** The college you ultimately want to earn your bachelor's degree from typically will have a feeder community college and a transfer program that supports that process. Ask the community college you choose about theirs and check out the transfer student office or program at the school you desire to get your bachelor's degree from. Contact both institutions so that you are clear on how the process works and what you need to do and have and by when. Once you earn your bachelor's degree, you can choose to take your community college off your resume or keep it. I think keeping it on your resume shows grit and that you're strategic about your decision-making.

6. **Manage Your Grades:** Getting a 4.0 GPA doesn't mean that you've won college. It means that you know how to follow directions really well. When is the last time you heard any of the world's most successful people say that they were the valedictorian of their class? Instead of trying to maximize your grades in every class, manage them. Strategically choose the classes you want to get an A in based on how relevant they are to your future and choose the classes where a lower grade, like a B, is okay because they are irrelevant though they are required. Classes only make up 40% of the college experience. The real value of the traditional college is mostly outside of the classroom. After the age of 25, nobody will care what your GPA was, and very few people will care what it is immediately after graduation. What will matter is your Other 4.0 which is your personal capital, intellectual capital, social capital, and financial capital. Don't let classes get in the way of you growing your Other 4.0 and thus your chances of success in your career and life.

7. **Get Heavily Involved:** Act like you belong there. You're not late to the party. You're right on time and not in as

much debt. The real richness of the college experience is not the classes, sports teams, or parties—it is the programs, events, leadership experiences, and relationships. Take advantage of every resource and relationship on campus as if you're playing catch up. You don't have time to be a wallflower like a freshman with four years ahead of them. You must fully immerse yourself. Your movement will be similar to that of a tourist who visits a new city and takes more advantage of everything the city has to offer than the people who have lived there for years. Join clubs, national organizations, and activities that will develop your passion, leadership, and network. Study abroad. Go to conferences. Attend events with guest speakers and authors. Get involved in student leadership. Remember, college is a safe-to-fail environment, so use it to develop your leadership skills by participating in student government. If living on or near campus will help you get more involved, then I encourage you to do so at this time since you already saved two years of rent by living at home.

8. **Major In Your Passion:** Continue developing your passion into a skill or finding a problem you are passionate about during this time. To become an expert at something requires 10,000 hours of practice, which equals 20 hours/week, 50 weeks/year, for ten years. If you start now, you'll be an expert by 30. Treat your passion like your major and your college major like your minor.

9. **Maximize Your Student Loans:** I know this sounds counterintuitive. This is an advanced strategy only for people who have an extreme degree of financial self-discipline. This should only be used for a viable business idea, real estate investment, or additional skills-based or personal development education you want to participate in as a way of invest-

ing in yourself. Do not use this strategy for any other reason. Federal loans at 5.05% is the cheapest form of financing you will find at your age of this magnitude without having a history of credit or collateral to guarantee the loan. Use it to invest in yourself or your idea. Student loans are not good debt. Good debt is money that puts money back into your pocket directly. Student loans don't do that directly because your school doesn't guarantee you a job. However, a business venture that you start now and build up for 2-4 years could fund your life. A rental property you buy can house you and your friends while producing cash flow that covers the mortgage, utilities, property taxes, and insurance. Taking an additional class on how to code even if you're not a computer science major or how to do drop shipping even if you don't consider yourself to be an entrepreneur will pour into your mind and then into your pockets if you follow through. And any class, event, or program that will help you increase your degrees of self-mastery (e.g., public speaking, self-confidence, negotiations, goal setting, time management, money management) is worth its weight in gold.

If you got your hands on this book after starting college, it's okay. You can still start at step 6. But the way you've been approaching college minute-by-minute will have to change based on this new awareness of how to win college versus just finishing it. As I think about my four year old daughter, this will be our approach in addition to me teaching her everything in The Freedom School curriculum. A lot could change and will change in fourteen years and this strategy will be adapted accordingly.

THE AFTERWORD

For Upperclassmen, Recent Graduates & Graduate
Students

If I Could Do It All Over Again Now

First and foremost, it is not too late. The principles I've
shared in this book, like *The Other 4.0*, are lifelong principles.
You're likely still in your 20s. You have time. Don't think "I wish I
read this as a freshman." Instead, just start now.

It's so easy to go with the flow and find yourself deferring your
dreams year after year after year. There seems to be a suggested
sequence for how we should live our lives and achieve success, but
my life has shown me that this isn't always the best path. Should you

buy a home before getting married? How long should you rent? Should you look for the highest paying job out of college or start at the bottom rung of a career you love? Should you buy an income property first or a single-family home? When is the right time to buy a new car? When is the best time to start building your company?

Below are 21 ways you could be hustling backward:

1. Buying a car you can't afford to maintain (I did this)

2. Buying a home you can't afford to maintain—beyond the mortgage there are lots of other expenses such as homeowner's insurance, taxes, roof work, plumbing work, cleaning, etc.

3. Increasing your cost of living based on your salary (which is not your income) and the assumption that your salary will always increase accordingly

4. Increasing your cost of living and paying for it with debt

5. Increasing your cost of living based on the income you're getting at a job you hate, when the income on the career path you desire may be (a lot) less

6. Not even knowing what your cost of living is

7. Letting money sit in a savings account earning a measly interest rate—with inflation, you might as well be throwing money away

8. Quitting your job instead of using your job while seriously testing out the economic viability of your business idea

9. Not knowing how to make money outside of the context of a job

10. Undercharging for what you make or do in fear of losing

low-paying price-sensitive probably-not-loyal clients

11. Saying you want to retire early, but not knowing your numbers—the number you need to save and the income you need to generate monthly once you retire

12. Taking on debt to buy a home or car or anything else that doesn't create more money than your loan payment

13. Taking on more "good" debt to go to graduate school because you're "supposed to" or don't know what else to do and not having a clear career plan on how to get a return on your investment as soon as possible afterward

14. Buying a single-family home and assuming it is an investment without it being a fixer-upper that you know will increase in value as you work on it or using Airbnb to help you create income with it

15. Buying or leasing a car that looks cool but does nothing positive for your asset or revenue column

16. Renting an overpriced apartment in an up-and-coming neighborhood when more affordable options exist, or you could be owning for the same amount

17. Taking expensive vacations to get away from a job you hate instead of investing in an idea that will free you from the job you hate

18. Spending $30,000 on a one-day wedding instead of making a down payment on a piece of property or other assets that will support your family forever

19. Using credit cards to buy things without setting up automatic withdrawal from your checking account so that you build your credit instead of killing it

20. Trusting that the stock market will automatically grow your money at 10% a year without you having to do anything when instead your own ideas can turn 10 cents into 11 cents (10% growth) in 12 months with the right amount of effort

21. Having more than two TVs in your home, not because the TVs cost too much, but because of how much the time you watch them costs you and your business ideas

There were many key decisions that I made in my 20s that contributed to my freedom today. While the decisions ahead of you may be different, I want to share some of the small decisions I made that ended up having a significant impact. Even if you're not in your 20s, similar decisions you make will either stall or throttle your journey to freedom over the next one or two decades.

Here are some of the intentional choices I made about my life that accelerated my freedom:

- Graduated from UCLA in three years, instead of four, saving thousands of dollars in student loans and starting my career faster. I had to take summer classes plus an extra class per quarter to do so.

- Applied to become Director of a program I worked for during college even though I was competing against people who appeared to be more qualified. I got the job managing about 30 employees and a decent size annual budget which accelerated my leadership experience.

- Read hundreds of books outside of class as if they were for class.

- Did most of the things in the *101 Things To Do Before You Graduate* book.

- Applied to the Stanford Graduate School of Business at the age of 23 making me one of the youngest in my class.

- Skipped my MBA summer internship and on-campus recruiting and used that time to build my company.

- Maximized my student loans to pour into my business since that was the easiest form of capital for me to access at the time.

- Raised additional money in exchange for equity for a dot com I was starting so I wasn't bearing all the financial risks.

- Took a bridge job at a small non-profit after graduation instead of a big-name consulting, banking, tech, or consumer products company that would have sucked up all of my time.

- Declared in advance of accepting my job my "quit criteria" (18 months on the job or 6 months of living expenses saved) which forced me to focus on my business in the mornings and evenings .

- Built my company as a side hustle while working a full-time job so that I didn't build it out of a sense of fear and scarcity.

- After proving myself and gaining the trust of my manager, I requested to work from 6:00 am to 3:00 pm instead of 9:00 am to 5:00 pm, which shortened my commute both ways, allowed me to be extremely productive for them from 6:00 am to 8:00 am since the office was empty, and gave me the chance to get home early and nap so I could wake up at 5:00 pm when everyone else was just getting off and work on my business from 5:00 pm until 10:00 pm.

- Created assets immediately by turning my frameworks into products and services.

- Created a blog to share my journey and ideas and published weekly.

- Lived like a college student, had a roommate, and kept my cost of living as low as possible for as long as possible until I had enough capital to make the moves I wanted.

- Waited to have kids until the path of my purpose was more solid and financially predictable.

- Had an inexpensive wedding with 60 guests and inexpensive wedding rings. We only asked for money as gifts. The real ring was the key ring to our multi-family home.

- Waited to buy a 3-family home that would pay for itself instead of buying a single-family home earlier.

- Bought a used 2000 Honda Accord with 95,000+ miles on it for $3,000 to run errands in 2013 instead of a newer car.

- Held off on costly vacations by creating a life that I didn't need to vacation from and building a business that allowed me to get paid to travel.

Each of these decisions accelerated my path to freedom. The two dumbest decisions I made were around cars. When I was 18, I bought a used Mercedes Benz for $3,500, but I didn't have enough money saved or coming in to maintain it. Thankfully, it was stolen two weeks after I bought it. That decision almost cost me my life. And upon getting my first job after graduation, I bought a used 3-year old Ford Mustang from Enterprise Rental Car Sales for around $15,000 despite only earning about $30,000 per year. Granted, it was broken down into monthly payments, but the price of your car should never be half of your annual salary. In between the Mercedes and the Mustang, I had two older Nissan Maximas, and I think I got fed up with older used cars and felt that I deserved something newer. These two choices are the only two I would really take back if I could.

MY 2003 UCLA AFRIKAN GRADUATION SPEECH

When I was an undergraduate student at UCLA, I began to sense the corruption of college. While I couldn't articulate it to the degree that I can now, the sentiment was the basis of my 2003 graduation speech. Now that I'm on the outside looking in and have some distance, I've written *The Undergrad Railroad* which digs deeper into the problem and the student's psyche than a 60-minute speech can. After traveling the country and speaking at over 100 colleges nationwide, I now know that it wasn't just me feeling this way. After my speeches, students line up to tell me how I put what they were feeling into words.

The book that opened my eyes during college was Carter G. Woodson's *The Mis-Education of the Negro*. I want this to be the modern day version of that classic. Over a decade and a half later, colleges haven't changed and the problem has only gotten worse. I'm also aware that the problem is not a Black problem—colleges don't discriminate. It's beyond Black and White—it's all about green.

Below is my 2013 UCLA Afrikan Graduation speech. I thought the imagery and poetry would be the perfect way to end this book.

===

Sunday, June 15, 2003
Royce Hall at UCLA

Welcome. In addition to my own father, there is another father I'd like to honor today, and his name is Steve Biko. Steve Biko is the father and martyr of the Black Consciousness Movement in South Africa. Though he has passed on, his ideas live on, and you will not only hear them, but you will also see them reflected in my speech.

My speech is entitled "Can You See What I See? (put on noose)

I want to know if you can see what I see?

This noose, which once draped the collars of our ancestors, has repositioned itself around our minds. Whereas it used to hang our ancestors from tree branches, now our future hangs in the balance.

Can you see the parallel? Can you see what I see?

During our K-12 education, many of our peers drowned in pages upon pages of impracticality and irrelevance. Middle school became a daunting Middle Passage. In the lower decks of the public education system, our youth huddle in classrooms for thirty by the forties.

Can you see the similarity? Can you see what I see?

234

Those lucky enough to acquire a higher education were our community's strongest candidates and most defiant leaders. Schools nationwide bid for us with pricey financial aid packages so that they could call us their own.

Can you see the analogy? Can you see what I see?

After commitments were made, these institutions stripped us from our homes, but rather than traveling by boat; we arrived by plane, car, and train. Untimely and in our prime, we were required to separate from our families who depended on us as much as we depended on them.

Can you see the comparison? Can you see what I see?

Upon arrival, we were mentally challenged to work harder than we ever worked before. Instead of picking cotton, we picked classes, however picking cotton seemed fruitful in comparison to choosing classes, unless we could find meaning in the material.

Can you see the resemblance? Can you see what I see?

The chancellor represents an executive authority, each building is a state, each classroom is a plantation, and each teacher owned each one of us, each quarter. Our campus is even divided into North and South campus, where the North represents liberal arts and sociology, and South campus represents logic and sciences. Post-Civil War American history can tell you where many of us spent most of our time.

Can you see the coincidence? Can you see what I see?

It's no coincidence that one of the most decorated degrees in education is called a masters, of which only a small percentage of African Americans hold.

So, if this is the case, then how do we prevent history from repeating itself?

Well, graduating with me today are 125 ways we can alter history.

Graduating with me today are 125 acts of defiance declaring that we reclaim our identity and re-write our forecasted destiny.

Today, we can remove this restraining rope (remove noose and hold high) as a statement of our mental freedom, for as Steve Biko said, "The most potent weapon in the hands of the oppressor is the mind of the oppressed."

Today we can celebrate, as we gather with our families and friends.

Today we can rejoice and thank God for helping us overcome.

Today we can observe the beauty of being Black.

I see today as our physical departure and our mental arrival, for we have made it through the unsettled waters of higher education.

I see our diplomas are more than purely paper.

I see our diplomas as self-written Emancipation Proclamations, proclaiming that today, we are free.

I see before me political leaders, athletes, artists, entrepreneurs, doctors, lawyers, engineers, and more.

I see sisterhood, brotherhood, family, and community.

I see a commitment to a common struggle to pursue a utopia that we will not likely see.

I see love, hope, prosperity, and potential.

And I even see tears of joy.

Close your eyes. See what you believe. And tell me, can you see what I see?

Thank you.

ENDNOTES

1. https://nces.ed.gov/programs/coe/indicator_ctr.asp

2. https://www.digitalcommerce360.com/article/e-commerce-sales-retail-sales-ten-year-review/

3. http://www.historynet.com/abolitionist-movement

4. https://www.rmc.edu/prospective-students/choosing-the-college-that-s-right-for-you/four-year-degree-guarantee

5. https://www.collegefactual.com/colleges/harvard-university/academic-life/graduation-and-retention/

6. https://www.collegefactual.com/colleges/stanford-university/academic-life/graduation-and-retention/

7. https://www.rmc.edu/offices/institutional-research/consumer-information

8. https://www.rmc.edu/about/four-year-degree-guarantee

9. http://www.ccdaily.com/2018/08/profits-face-fraud-complaints-devos-weakens-rules/

10. https://www.brookings.edu/research/the-looming-student-loan-default-crisis-is-worse-than-we-thought/

11. http://archive.washtenawvoice.com/wp-content/uploads/2012/07/campaign-e1342968267425.jpg

12. https://www.usnews.com/education/community-colleges/washtenaw-community-college-CC09054

13. https://www.highlands.edu/wp-content/uploads/2018/06/GHC6869-Billboard-Mockup.jpg

14. https://www.usnews.com/education/community-colleges/georgia-highlands-college-CC03144

15. https://www.highlands.edu/2018/06/21/ghc-advancement-team-brings-home-several-national-awards-collegiate-advertising-awards-educational-advertising-awards

16. https://i.pinimg.com/236x/f4/cc/87/f4cc875a850a423a89257f-b889b4b782--billboard-design-thomas-jefferson.jpg

17. https://www.devry.edu/d/graduation-rates.pdf

18. https://www.csun.edu/sites/default/files/styles/slideshow_full/public/field_image/field_slideshow_slides/new_brand_V2_0_0.jpg?itok=9Z-HqzEG

19. https://www.collegefactual.com/colleges/california-state-university-northridge/outcomes/

20. https://mir-s3-cdn-cf.behance.net/project_modules/disp/9dee5c19477889.562db170dc582.jpg

21. https://www.usnews.com/education/community-colleges/rio-salado-college-CC07226

22. https://www.forbes.com/sites/zackfriedman/2017/02/21/student-loan-debt-statistics-2017/#4f6f02b05dab

23. https://www.usnews.com/education/best-colleges/articles/how-us-news-calculated-the-rankings

24. https://www.dailymail.co.uk/news/article-3075189/High-school-graduates-earn-1-million-lifetime-graduate-college-new-report-finds.html

25. http://www.cracked.com/blog/5-ways-college-screws-over-poor-kids

26. https://www.alternet.org/revealed-state-colleges-giving-wealthy-kids-more-financial-aid-poor-kids

27. https://studentloanhero.com/student-loan-debt-statistics/

28. https://studentaid.ed.gov/sa/types/loans/interest-rates

29. https://nslds.ed.gov/nslds/nslds_SA/defaultmanagement/search_-cohort_2015_CY.cfm

30. https://en.wikipedia.org/wiki/Sallie_Mae

31. https://nces.ed.gov/programs/coe/indicator_ctr.asp

32. https://nces.ed.gov/programs/coe/indicator_ctr.asp

33. https://www.collegefactual.com/colleges/university-of-california-los-angeles/outcomes/

34. https://www.washingtonpost.com/news/wonk/wp/2013/05/20/only-27-percent-of-college-grads-have-a-job-related-to-their-major/?noredirect=on&utm_term=.15d6f116f787

35. http://www.vox.com/2016/5/23/11704246/wealth-inequality-cartoon

36. https://www.credible.com/blog/calculators/student-loan-calculator

37. http://time.com/money/collection-post/3829776/heres-what-the-average-grad-makes-right-out-of-college/

38. https://www.payscale.com/research/US/School=Harvey_Mudd_College/Salary

39. https://nces.ed.gov/programs/digest/d17/tables/dt17_330.10.asp

40. http://www.pewresearch.org/fact-tank/2017/02/15/u-s-students-internationally-math-science/

41. https://ucla.app.box.com/v/acct-pdf-AFR-16-17

42. http://facts.stanford.edu/administration/finances

43. https://www.nyu.edu/content/dam/nyu/financialOperationsTreas/documents/financial_statements/NYU-CFS-2017.pdf

44. https://truthout.org/articles/the-art-of-the-gouge-nyu-as-a-model-for-predatory-higher-education/

45. https://www.moreheadstate.edu/getattachment/Administration/Accounting-Financial-Services/Forms-Resources/Audit-Reports/2018-Issued-Single-Audit-Financial-Statements.pdf.aspx?lang=en-US

46. https://www.insidehighered.com/news/2016/06/07/where-was-class-2015-six-months-after-graduation

47. https://www.huffingtonpost.co.uk/2016/01/07/ernst-and-young-removes-degree-classification-entry-criteria_n_7932590.html?guccounter=1&guce_referrer_us=aHR0cHM6Ly93d3cuZ29v-Z2xlLmNvbS8&guce_referrer_cs=D3S1gmLvxmpjNRlJMu29lg

48. https://www.bustle.com/articles/151243-how-the-price-of-college-has-changed-since-our-parents-were-in-school

49. https://www.bloomberg.com/news/articles/2014-08-18/college-tuition-costs-soar-chart-of-the-day

50. https://www.infoplease.com/us/higher-education/number-us-colleges-and-universities-and-degrees-awarded-2005

51. https://money.cnn.com/2013/06/24/pf/emergency-savings/index.html

52. https://money.cnn.com/2017/12/18/technology/uber-drivers-180-days-of-change/index.html

53. http://fortune.com/fortune500/list/

54. http://www.experian.com/blogs/ask-experian/graduates-and-credit

55. https://www.capitalone.com/credit-cards/journey-student

56. https://blog.equifax.com/credit/can-one-late-payment-affect-my-credit-score/

57. https://blog.equifax.com/credit/can-one-late-payment-affect-my-credit-score/

58. https://www.creditkarma.com/trends/age

59. https://wallethub.com/credit-cards/no-credit-student/

60. http://www.marketwatch.com/story/nearly-4-out-of-5-students-work-2013-08-07

61. https://cew.georgetown.edu/wp-content/uploads/Press-release-WorkingLearners__FINAL.pdf

62. https://www.irs.com/articles/2018-federal-tax-rates-personal-exemptions-and-standard-deductions

63. https://www.bls.gov/tus/charts/students.htm

64. https://nces.ed.gov/fastfacts/display.asp?id=372

65. https://www.forbes.com/sites/prestoncooper2/2017/12/19/college-completion-rates-are-still-disappointing/#6479e6d7263a

Made in the USA
Columbia, SC
13 February 2020